SpellCraft
FOR TEENS

A MAGICKAL GUIDE TO WRITING & CASTING SPELLS

What Is Magick?

Magick is the art of using positive energy to focus your will and create positive and useful change. Spells are not meant to solve all your problems, but they can help you find answers and achieve goals, and will influence your life in a positive and meaningful way.

I use Wiccan Magick (sometimes called White Witchcraft) to help others as well as myself. Spells can be cast for all kinds of purposes, but in Wicca there is a rule called the Rede, which states, "An ye harm none, do what ye will." This rule is the most important thing to learn, know, and follow when it comes to any and all Magick.

As you hold this book in your hands, you hold the power to mold, change, and shape your life. If you follow your heart and adhere to the Rede, then you can unleash the Witch within and discover the power of Magick.

About the Author

Gwinevere Rain is a hip, stylish, teenage Witch. She's been practicing Wicca since the age of fourteen, and is firmly dedicated to helping fellow teens build self-confidence and inner spiritual love. Gwinevere is an avid reader and writer of the Craft.

In her spare time she loves to dabble with potions, powders, and lotions, and she also creates mystical, magickal products for her own online witchy store.

Always remember Gwinevere's motto: "Love the Goddess, love yourself, and love life!"

To Write to the Author

If you wish to contact the author or would like more information about this book, please write to the author in care of Llewellyn Worldwide and we will forward your request. Both the author and publisher appreciate hearing from you and learning of your enjoyment of this book and how it has helped you. Llewellyn Worldwide cannot guarantee that every letter written to the author can be answered, but all will be forwarded. Please write to:

Gwinevere Rain
℅ Llewellyn Worldwide
P.O. Box 64383, Dept. 0-7387-0225-0
St. Paul, MN 55164-0383, U.S.A.
Please enclose a self-addressed stamped envelope for reply,
or $1.00 to cover costs. If outside U.S.A., enclose
international postal reply coupon.

Many of Llewellyn's authors have websites with additional information and resources. For more information, please visit our website at:
http://www.llewellyn.com

SpellCraft
FOR TEENS

A MAGICKAL GUIDE TO WRITING & CASTING SPELLS

GWINEVERE RAIN

2002
Llewellyn Publications
St. Paul, Minnesota 55164-0383, U.S.A.

First Edition
Second Printing, 2002

Book design by Donna Burch
Cover art and interior illustrations © 2002 by Mister Reusch
Cover design by Gavin Dayton Duffy
Editing by Karin Simoneau

Library of Congress Cataloging-in-Publication Data

Rain, Gwinevere, 1984–
    Spellcraft for teens : a magickal guide to writing & casting spells / Gwinevere Rain.
        p.   cm.
    Includes bibliographical references.
    ISBN 0-7387-0225-0
       1. Magic. 2. Charms. 3. Witchcraft. I. Title

    BF1611 .R14 2002
    133.4'3—dc21   2002067105

Llewellyn Worldwide does not participate in, endorse, or have any authority or responsibility concerning private business transactions between our authors and the public.

All mail addressed to the author is forwarded but the publisher cannot, unless specifically instructed by the author, give out an address or phone number.

Any Internet references contained in this work are current at publication time, but the publisher cannot guarantee that a specific location will continue to be maintained. Please refer to the publisher's website for links to authors' websites and other sources.

Llewellyn Publications
A Division of Llewellyn Worldwide, Ltd.
P.O. Box 64383, Dept. 0-7387-0225-0
St. Paul, MN 55164-0383, U.S.A.
www.llewellyn.com

 Printed in the United States of America on recycled paper

Dedicated to young Witches everywhere—
may your magickal journey be blessed with courage,
love, and friendship.

Acknowledgments

Many blessings and thanks to my family and friends. To my mother for endlessly supporting all my endeavors; and to Seetal and Maggie, my crazy, beautiful, best friends for filling my days with laughter and keeping all my silly secrets.

To Dragon Storm, for believing in me always; to Midnight Grey Wolfpup, editor of Cauldrons-Broomsticks.net, for giving me the opportunity to express myself, grow, and learn throughout the years, seasons, and Sabbats; and to Scott Cunningham, whose words taught me the ways of Wicca and led me to the Goddess' open and waiting arms.

To Megan Atwood, Karin Simoneau, and the fabulous Llewellyn staff, for taking a chance on a young writer and Witch with a dream. And finally, to my Goddess and God, Lord and Lady, for giving me many magickal gifts.

Thank you again to those listed above, and anyone I may have missed. I am amazingly blessed by your bountiful friendship, support, and guidance!

Book Blessing
Earth, Air, Fire & Water

I call to the greenest north—
north of earth, birthing, starting, caring;
I call to the enchanted east—
east of air, flying, bringing, whistling;
I call to the silent south—
south of fire, blazing, burning, growing;
I call to the Witch's west—
west of water, cleansing, blessing, knowing;
I conjure and summon,
cast forth my desire,
by the all mighty powers of
earth, air, fire, water;
bewitch and bless all that is.
So be it now!

Contents

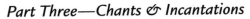

Contents

Part Four—Bewitching: Correspondences & Magickal Properties

Part Five—A Witch's Journal & Magickal Record Keeping

preface

If you've ever been engrossed in a magickal fairytale, watched a movie about Witchcraft, or craved the power to cast a spell . . . this book is for you. I have never seen Magick, but I've felt it. Magick is the tingle in my fingertips, the wind blowing through my hair, and the storm that brews in the dark approaching clouds. Magick is the energy of life. It's everywhere and in everything.

To cast a Magick spell is to take the reins and take control of your life. Anyone can be a Witch and cast a spell—you don't have to belong to a coven and there are no age restrictions. And if you've heard that only females can be Witches, you've heard wrong!

Whether you've been practicing Magick for a little while, or you're just discovering it, you may have heard (or eventually will hear) someone say, "You must write your own spells; they are more powerful." Although this isn't necessary, in a way it's true—writing your own spells enhances the Magick because you put your energy into it from start to finish. Also, you pick the ingredients, so you spend less time running around looking for exotic magickal herbs that most spell books recommend you use.

So, writing your own spells is better, but there are a whole bunch of drawbacks that seem to make things a bit complicated. I have heard all the excuses: "I can't write my own spells because I don't know where to start," "It takes too much time and research," "I don't have the books or resources," and, my all-time favorite, "I can't rhyme!"

Someone once said, "Behind every problem lies a solution." Well, the solution is in your hands, literally. *SpellCraft for Teens* will take you step by step through the entire writing and casting process. Most of the research has already been done, meaning you probably won't need additional books or resources. With this book, writing a spell will take you half the time it would normally take. If you can't rhyme, that's O.K., because all the chants and incantations have been written for you!

It is rather tempting to skip this whole process and reach for a spell book, but there are drawbacks to using them as well. Here are five reasons you may want to throw your spell books out the window: (1) you often don't have or can't find a particular herb that you need; (2) you did not put the energy into writing the spells; (3) some of the listed ingredients and herbs are expensive; (4) you don't like the spells because they aren't original or unique; or (5) the spells may call for candles, which you might not be able to use.

SpellCraft for Teens provides a list of easy-to-find herbs for each magickal purpose. You will have to do some work, but this work will provide you with a great sense of accomplishment once the spell is complete. Most of the ingredients and equipment (such as basil, cinnamon, or small safety pins) can be found around the house. The spells you create will be original and unique because you made them, brewing each spell till it is just right. Candle Magick is discussed in this book; if you are not able to use candles, there are sections on knot Magick, conjuring bags, and poppets.

Where other spell books have failed, *SpellCraft for Teens* will succeed. Within these pages you will learn real Magick by casting real spells that you have written, and you will see real results.

Introduction

Stories, movies, and old tales tell us of Witches, potions, and Magick spells. When I was younger, I wondered if the stories were true . . . no, wait . . . I wondered if Witches were real. As I grew older, logic began to kick in. *They can't be real, Witches don't exist, there are no such things,* I thought. Only later, when I was in ninth grade, did I learn how wrong I really was.

A few events in my life led me to start researching spells and Magick. When I look back, I realize that it wasn't one thing in particular that piqued my interest, but rather a variety of things. What I discovered was so profound, so awesome, that it changed my life: Magick is real! But there was more. I discovered a religion whose members believe in Magick and honor not one, but two deities—the Goddess and the God. This unique faith is now my religion, and it's called Wicca.

My family is Catholic, and when I was little I went to church every now and then. Others in my class went to religious education classes, but I did not. Religion was present in my life, yes, but it wasn't really a focal point. Besides, at age eight or nine, theology and religious philosophy didn't exactly interest me.

You could say I have always been a Witch at heart. When I was young, my mother would read me Greek myths out of fabulous picture books. Once I was able to read on my own, I read *Dora the Witch* books. I also had a weird connection with the moon; it was (and still is) utterly breathtaking. Then there was the movie *The Wizard of Oz,* or, more specifically, Glenda the Good Witch. She was beautiful, had a Magick wand, and flew in a bubble! What more could you ask for? Witchcraft was in the back of my mind, itching to get out!

In ninth grade, I wasn't Ms. Popular, but I did have a few friends; my best friend was Seetal. She, by the way, thought I was joking when I told her I was a Witch. You know, high school is hard, and being a teenager these days is much more complicated than most adults think. We deal with everything from friends and family to teachers and tons of school work. There is always something to worry about: maintaining a good reputation, putting up with obnoxious classmates, and the list goes on and on. Sometimes I think it's a miracle we survive! Wicca and Magick took my mind off all that stuff. It was a distraction that was welcomed. I spent an hour a day on the Internet reading and taking notes. Witchcraft completely fascinated me.

One woman, Astara, whom I trusted and e-mailed frequently, suggested I read a book called *Wicca: A Guide for the
Solitary Practitioner,* by Scott Cunningham. I went to the book-
store and picked up a copy. I absolutely loved it! I believe everyone has an inner
compass—some force within that guides us to the right path. After reading that
book, my inner being, my soul, was shouting *This is right!* From that point on I
no longer looked at Wicca as just some religion, but as *my* religion.

Magick is the art of using positive energy to focus your will and create positive and useful change. Spells are not meant to solve all your problems, but they
can help you find answers, achieve goals, and they can influence your life in a
positive and meaningful way. Magick is a catalyst for transformation, so
be ready to kick out the old and bring in the new. You may be wondering
why I am spelling Magick with a *k*. Most of us witchy people spell Magick
with a *k* because it helps show the difference between stage magic (magic
with a *c*) and Magick spells.

I use Wiccan Magick (sometimes called White Witchcraft) to help others as
well as myself. Spells can be cast for all kinds of purposes, but in Wicca there is
a rule called the Rede, which states, "An ye harm none, do what ye will." This
rule is the most important thing to learn, know, and follow when it
comes to any and all Magick.

As you hold this book in your hands, you hold the power to
mold, change, and shape your life. If you follow your heart and adhere to the Rede, then you can unleash the Witch within and discover the power of Magick.

Part One

Living Magickally:
The Wiccan Path

Wicca

Perhaps one of the hardest things for a person to do is to write about her own faith. Where to start? What do I say and how am I going to say it? These are the questions running through my mind, the obstacles that tower before me. The truth is, Wicca can't be fully described in a few short pages. For this reason, many books are limited to the topic of Wiccan practices. Later, I will provide you with a comprehensive list of great books about Wicca that are more in depth.

On the following pages you will read a little bit about Wicca. It is a religion legally recognized by the United States government. This means that if you choose to become Wiccan you are protected by the First Amendment, which basically says that you have the freedom to follow any religious path.

Wicca is a contemporary religion with a belief in two deities: the Goddess and the God. It is usually defined as a new or modern religious path. But although Wicca is rather new, the belief in and worship of dual deities, masculine and feminine, is as old as civilization itself. The changing of seasons and harvest celebrations are ancient practices, which Wiccans partake in yearly. So the religion of Wicca may be new, but the beliefs and concepts are a rebirth of the ancient ways.

This unique spiritual path doesn't have a designated holy book or scripture; instead, Wiccans flow with the rhythm of life, and follow two rules: the Wiccan Rede and the Rule of Three. The Wiccan Rede conveys a message of harming none, and the rule of three stresses a karmic effect, meaning the energies you send out into the world you receive back threefold. These two guidelines are taken seriously and are applied to everyday life as well as to magickal castings.

There is more to Wicca than magickal rites. Wiccans worship the Goddess and God and honor them during seasonal holidays, called *Sabbats*. The Sabbats consist of the two equinoxes, the two solstices, and four other lesser holidays. Samhain, the last of the three harvests (the first two being Lammas and Mabon) is undertaken on the wicked day of October 31, also known as Halloween. Samhain is celebrated as a harvest, but the symbolism

4

behind this facade represents death—death of negative thinking, death of anger, and, in mythology, death of the Sun God.

Each Sabbat represents something, such as a harvest or the coming of spring, but in the same way, each also tells a story filled with ancient mythology and evocative symbolism. All Sabbats lead to the common theme of life, death, and rebirth, seen throughout Wicca in many different ways. The Sabbats call for celebration. Some Wiccans gather together and feast, while others hold a private, solitary ritual.

The eight Sabbats are as follows:

Imbolc: February 2

Ostara (vernal equinox): around March 21

Beltane: April 30

Midsummer (summer solstice): around June 21

Lammas: August 1

Mabon (autumnal equinox): around September 21

Samhain: October 31

Yule (winter solstice): around December 21

It goes without saying that the holidays are sacred and positive. No devil-worshipping or evil sacrifices occur during Sabbat rituals or any other Wiccan ritual.

Many faiths have creation myths, and in Wicca there are several. However, these myths are mainly used for their symbolism. It is said that there once existed a being called "the All," which consisted of both masculine and feminine attributes. It then split itself in half, creating two separate deities—the Goddess and the God. From there the earth was

6 formed and human life was born. Whenever I think about this theory, my mind conjures up the image of the yin-yang symbol. This Taoist symbol represents a masculine half and a feminine half coming together, which in essence is what "the All" really is.

Psychologists say each of us has a masculine and feminine side. In relation to Wicca, each of us has a Goddess and God within. We are all equal and sacred beings, no matter what our race, gender, religion, and so on. This common belief gives Wiccans the power to overcome prejudice and hatred.

Many Wiccans practice Magick. To cast Magick we utilize certain tools, work according to the moon's phases, and perform spells within a sacred circle. A Wiccan who practices the Craft alone is called a *solitary practitioner*. Others gather together to celebrate the Sabbats and work various rituals and magickal rites. This group is called a *coven*. Solitary work is a bit different from coven work, but both strive to accomplish the same things and both adhere to similar rules.

Wicca is a very nature-oriented path. The moon is symbolic of the Goddess and the sun is symbolic of the God. Each practitioner sees things in a slightly different way; for the most part, all of us are looking to grasp control of our lives and cut new paths in the road. Wicca is always changing, growing, and evolving, which is a good thing!

Witches, Wiccans, and the Magickal

Can you practice Magick and follow another religion? Is it possible (or fair) to blend Wicca with another religious path? Is there a difference between Wicca and Witchcraft? These questions have been the topic of many conversations and debates.

Magick does not belong to any one religious path. In fact, Wicca is just one of many groups whose members practice some form of Magick. Shamans, voodoo practitioners, ancient Egyptians, and Native Americans are other groups that come to mind.

It is not my place to say that there is only one way or path. I believe there are many ways to reach the higher powers (whomever you believe them to be). Blending Wicca with another religion is a personal choice. Is it possible? Yes. Is it fair? Honestly, I just don't know. The option is there, but if you choose to blend, expect some controversy. As long as you know in your heart that it is the correct path for you, then that is the only thing that matters.

Is there a difference between Wicca and Witchcraft? In my opinion there is. The fact of the matter is that there are not many books that address this issue. My definitions of Wicca and Witchcraft may not be agreed upon by all, but hopefully I will help you understand the difference, and clarify the confusion.

Talk of Witchcraft has been around for centuries, but it is hard to produce evidence that there were generations of Witches who practiced the Craft. The inability to be public about the Craft led to little record keeping or organization. Witchcraft is the art and practice of Magick. Depending on the individual's definition and how she chooses to label her path, Witchcraft may or may not be a religion. The label of "Witch" is so general it can relate to almost anyone on the magickal path. Both males and females are identified as Witches. The word "warlock" is not used because it disparages and offends the male practitioner.

Wicca is a rather new word, although some say it branches off from older words such as *Wis,* an Old English word meaning "wise," or *Wita,* which is Old English for "councilor." Wicca is a religion that molds contemporary Witchcraft with the seasons, elements, Sabbats, gods, and sacred rituals; it is a religion that has moral and ethical guidelines. Wiccans use Witchcraft (the art and practice of Magick) to create change within their lives. Because Wiccans utilize Witchcraft, every Wiccan is a Witch. When I use the term "Witchcraft" in this book, I refer to the magickal aspect of Wicca.

Some practitioners use Witchcraft and Wicca interchangeably, and this doesn't necessarily mean they are incorrect. Here it gets a bit complicated, but let me explain: Before the word "Wicca" came into popular use, older, more seasoned practitioners identified their belief system as Witchcraft. Yet when one analyzes her path, the beliefs are pretty much identical to Wicca. This is one of my reasons for stating that Witchcraft may or may not be a religion—to some it is a religion.

Others identify themselves as Witches because (1) they don't agree with the Wiccan philosophy, (2) they don't believe that Witchcraft is a religion so they practice Magick and follow another religion (Catholicism or Judaism, for example), or (3) they were raised in a family that practiced Witchcraft. All these labels and names aren't nearly as important as what you, the magickal reader, believe and follow. It isn't the name of your path—it's what your path means to you. As long as you believe in some positive guiding force, you've got a good start!

The Witches' Rune

A pentagram is a five-pointed star. The points represent Spirit (also called *Akasha*) and the four elements—earth, air, fire, and water. A pentacle is a pentagram encased within a circle. When the pentacle is shown upright, it represents positive energies, which Wiccans tap into for protection, power, and guidance.

10 Both symbols (the pentacle and the pentagram) are used to represent the Wiccan faith. They do not represent evil or the devil in any way.

Sometimes (especially in my chants and incantations) I refer to the pentacle as the Witches' Rune. Many Wiccan traditions utilize the symbol. Due to the fact that Wicca is so diverse, it makes the symbol all the more powerful because it is a uniting force among all that is magickal.

These symbols have many uses. The power is infinite. Below are some examples of how pentagrams and pentacles are commonly used:

- A pentagram can be drawn in the air above each element when invoking the corners, and once again in the opposite direction to release the corners.

- Pentacles can be worn as jewelry (most often necklaces) to bring the power of protection to the practitioner.

- Pentagrams and pentacles can be carved on a disk and placed on the altar to protect, bless, and consecrate items.

- A pentacle is often drawn on a sheet of paper and placed in a conjuring bag to bring about protection, purification, and power.

Practice, Persistence, and Faith

Even the most experienced Witches had to start somewhere. They practiced hard to achieve their wisdom, knowledge, and expertise. There is no secret formula or shortcut to becoming an experienced Witch. It's a journey that involves practice, persistence, and faith.

Practice

As with any craft, practice is necessary. By "practice," I mean reading and experimenting! Reading books about spells and Magick will help better your understanding and prepare you for casting, as will gathering information from various websites. Performing your first spell is a once-in-a-lifetime experience, because at this time you reaffirm what you already know—you are a Witch. One of the things I learned during my experimental period is that mistakes are bound to happen. Saying the wrong words or forgetting a tool is not so bad. The higher powers have a sense of humor, so don't worry about small mistakes. Another thing I learned is that writing and casting spells gradually becomes easier over time.

Persistence

Somebody once said, "If at first you don't succeed, try, try again." In Witchcraft it is an unwritten rule. Getting what you want is not going to come at the snap of your fingers, so persistence is the next best thing. You can accomplish anything you set your mind to. If you have a goal (one that won't harm anyone, of course), then do everything you can to make it happen. If you cast a spell and see no results in a month, give it another try . . . cast it again.

Faith

Having faith in yourself is just as important as having faith in the higher powers. Even if you are the most experienced Witch in the world, if you doubt your Magick, it won't work. How can you expect anything to work if *you* don't believe it will? Instead of asking yourself, *Will this work?* say to yourself, *When the time is right, it will manifest.* Back the spell up with positive thoughts and reassurance rather than doubts and negative feedback. If you can dream it and believe it, then with some hard work it will eventually come your way.

Craft Names

Have you ever despised your birth name so badly that you thought of inventing another one? I think everyone has wished for a new name at one point or another. In Wicca, practitioners have the option of creating new names for themselves. The purpose of a magickal or Craft name is not to deny or get rid of your given name, but to represent the birth of a new magickal you!

A Craft name is a symbol of your endeavor on to the Wiccan path. Craft names came to be because years ago there was a need to keep a Witch's identity a secret. During the horrible Witch persecutions, practitioners called each other by their Craft names only. They feared that if people discovered their real names, the persecutors would track them down and inflict harm. As you may have guessed, this is no longer a concern, fortunately.

Finding a Craft name will take time. If you choose something you outgrow, you can always change it. Some suggest allowing a Craft name to come to you. The name may come encoded in a dream or meditation, so be sure to pay close attention to any messages or symbols. You may want to look into numerology or make a list of your favorite things. Some Craft names reflect nature or the elements. If you're at a loss, sit down and seriously think about flowers, colors, stones, or animals with which you feel a connection. I strongly suggest that you take your time and select a Craft name that you really relate to and love. Your Craft name can be a few words combined together, such as "Mystic Gray Cat," or a simple, short, sweet name like "Moonstone."

Altar

An altar is a place of power where Wiccans worship, celebrate, and cast Magick. This religious table comes in all shapes and sizes. My altar is in my bedroom,

and I always leave it set up. Having a permanent altar is comforting because I can light candles, close my eyes, and feel at home any time.

But for the teen practitioner, having a permanent altar is not always an option. So what can you do? There are ways to mask an altar and hide it from plain view, or create it to blend in with the theme of your room. Also, you can set it up for rituals, spells, Sabbats, and so on, and put it away when not in use.

Letting your creative energies run wild and your intuition flow is the first step to creating an altar.

14 What the altar consists of is not nearly as important as what it represents. The altar is like a miniature Wiccan church, a personal place of worship.

The altar can be a small box, table, chest, shelf, or even a section of a dresser. A small cloth (one that is in proportion to the altar) is usually draped over the top. This altar cloth is not necessary, but if you are using an ugly box it will brighten it up.

What exactly goes on an altar? Representations (statues, candles, images, and so on) of the Goddess and God are positioned on the altar to show them respect and honor. Magickal tools like full moon blessed water, salt in a jar, a wand, candles, incense, and other items are placed on the altar, too. The broom is placed next to the altar, away from all candles.

The altar is a reflection of the self, because it reflects your positive and loving energies. It is the home of your sacred objects. Every time you use your altar, the tools will emanate and grow with power.

At first I thought my altar was boring. *What am I going to do with it?* I wondered. But after some time I realized that there are *so* many fun things to do with an altar! One of the first rituals you may want to do is an altar-blessing ritual, using one of the "blessing" incantations provided in this book. Following is a short list of cool ways to use an altar:

◆ If you can't cast a circle because of lack of time or room, perform a spell on the altar without a circle. This is a super witchy substitute!

◆ Leave flowers, rocks, and stones on the altar as an offering. This builds up the loving energy!

◆ Sit before the altar, light some candles and incense, and meditate about the day. This helps to reduce stress and calm the body.

◆ Write new spells in front of the altar. This connects you with the energy of the Goddess and God and helps the creative juices flow!

◆ Place jewelry, charms, and amulets on the altar for a few nights during the waxing or full moon phase. This empowers the items and sends surges of positive and protective energies throughout.

Magickal Tools

Witches use specific tools to cast circles and perform spells and sacred rituals. Most tools can be handmade. Others can be bought for a relatively low price. You don't need a one-hundred-dollar chalice (a ritual cup), but you may need a few candle holders, which can be found anywhere. The most important tool is you, the Witch. You send the energy into the tool, not the other way around!

Each of your tools should be respected as sacred objects. If you shove your Magick wand under the bed (a.k.a. the bottomless pit), it will probably accumulate dust instead of magickal energy. It takes time to build up a nice collection of tools, statues, and trinkets, so don't hesitate because you don't have all the tools you'd like to have. Listed on the following pages are some important tools you may want to use.

16 **Book of Shadows:** A Book of Shadows is a journal in which you keep all your magickal thoughts, spells, rituals, and information. At the end of this book you'll learn about creating and maintaining your own Book of Shadows.

Wand: The wand is an element of air, and its main purpose is to send energy from the Witch into an object or space. Specifically, wands are used when casting the Magick circle. Wands can be fashioned from sticks and decorated with crystals, symbols, and more. Making a wand isn't a hard task; in fact, it's great fun!

Full Moon Blessed Water: Full moon blessed water combines the powerful element of water and the Goddess' lunar energy. It can be utilized to cleanse and purify the practitioner, tools, and anything you desire! (My recipe for full moon blessed water can be found on page 19.)

Candles: Candles are part of the element of fire. They are commonly used in Magick spells as representations of the deities and as a source of illumination. Candles serve many purposes, but they can be dangerous. Read the candle safety section beginning on page 20 before using this tool.

Cauldron (fireproof container): The cauldron is associated with Witches as much as brooms are associated with them. Although cauldrons aren't used to boil deadly potions, they are used to divine the future, hold fire (when performing outdoor rituals), and catch ashes from paper that is lit on fire during a particular spell. Some cauldrons can be pricey, but if you look hard enough you can find one that is affordable. Although it isn't the prettiest looking substitute, an empty coffee can will work marvelously!

Salt: Salt grains (table salt or sea salt) can be used for many magickal purposes. Salt has cleansing attributes as well as protective properties. I usually keep a jar of salt next to a jar of full moon blessed water. Both are true essentials in Wiccan Magick.

Broom: A broom is also referred to as a besom. The broom is used to symbolically sweep the circle and purify sacred space. Although it is not completely necessary, it is one of my favorite tools.

Music: Listening to a calming CD or tape while performing a spell really helps the practitioner get into the ritual mood. I enjoy listening to the sounds of the ocean, and I also listen to Enya.

Following are more tools you can use. However, the aforementioned tools are, in my opinion, essentials, while those listed on the following page are optional. Remember, some tools are more expensive than others, so try to collect the ones that you feel are absolutely necessary.

18

Athame: An athame is a dull ritual knife that is commonly used as an instrument to cast a circle. It should never be used to hurt another. (I prefer to use a wand when I cast my circle.)

Chalice: The chalice is a ritual cup that is used during Sabbats and specific rituals. Some covens have feasting within the circle, and the chalice (which typically contains wine or juice) is passed around the circle so the practitioners can drink from it. The liquid is usually consecrated in a specific fashion.

Altar Pentacle: The altar pentacle is used to bless and consecrate ritual tools.

Drum: The drum is used in some traditions to raise energy within the circle.

Bell: The bell can be rung to invoke the eastern corner during the circle casting. It has female energies, and it is occasionally used to banish negative energies.

A Ritual to Make
Full Moon Blessed Water

Moon Phase: full moon

You will need:

> One small jar filled with tap water (a bowl or cup will work, too)
> Salt
> Piece of paper

Save the blessed water and use to bless candles, Magick cords, and other tools. Every full moon, spill out the old water and create fresh water! If you'd like, cast a Magick circle and perform this ritual.

Place the jar on the center of the paper.

Put your hands above your head and place your palms together. Say:

> *"Hail fair moon,*
> *please, aid me in my task.*
> *Bless thy water with your power."*

Sprinkle a bit of salt in a circle (clockwise motion, of course) around the jar (on the paper). Place your hands over the jar; close your eyes and visualize a bright white light around it. Say:

"By the powers above and thy blessed full moon,
this water is now purified and consecrated for all magickal workings!"

Clap three times and say in a strong voice:

"As I will it,
so mote it be."

It's done!
Now you can use your full moon blessed water!

Types of Candles and Safety Tips

Candles come in all different shapes and sizes! Some common candles you may have heard about include tapers, votives, four-inch mini-spell candles, and tealights. These easy-to-find candles are used by Witches to cast funky and cool spells.

Candle Magick is fun, effective, and easy to use, but it can be dangerous if you don't know what you're doing. This is why it is extremely important to learn proper candle safety. First, let's look at the different types of candles that you might consider using, then we'll move on to learning about candle safety.

Tapers are tall, thin candles that range in height from six to twelve inches. Votives are about three-inches tall and are wider. Mini-spell candles are rather thin, four inches high, and can be a bit difficult to locate (they are mainly found in witchy/metaphysical stores). Tealights are inexpensive candles that already come in foiled holders. They are about one-inch high and are about the same width as votive candles.

Tapers can easily tip over, so, if possible, work with votives, tealights, and/or spell candles (if you can find them). Also, note that there are other types of candles available, and gradually (if you're allowed to use candles) you'll branch out into other unique shapes and sizes. When choosing candles, keep in mind the height of the candle. Remember . . . the taller it is the more easily it can tip over.

Each lit candle must have its own candle holder—no ifs, ands, or buts! Try to purchase two matching votive candle holders; there really shouldn't be a need for more. Candle safety doesn't stop at purchasing holders. You must always be on guard, and make sure the surface on which you place the candle isn't wobbly, slanted, or flammable.

Keep a large cup of water nearby. This is a small measure of insurance that is both helpful and smart. Mentally plan a specific course of action to take should something tip over. Talk with your parents beforehand about safety guidelines or rules they may have when working with candles.

Lastly, be smart! Just because you're performing Magick doesn't mean you should throw caution to the wind. Following are more candle

22

safety tips. Read through the list before every candle Magick casting and, if possible, commit the list to memory.

◆ Don't place candles near any curtains.

◆ Roll up sleeves, tie up hair, and don't let any clothing hang over candles.

◆ Keep water nearby, and come up with a safety plan in case an accident does happen.

◆ If a candle flame gets too high and jumpy, extinguish it, then tell the candle you're sorry.

◆ If you plan on meditating, light one candle instead of several. With only one candle burning, there is less chance of an accident happening while your eyes are closed.

◆ Start out with one or two candles, then gradually increase the number of candles you work with.

To extinguish candles, some practitioners say that you must snuff out the candle with a designated candle snuffer. As every Witch is different and unique, I have found that blowing them out works best for me. I have a couple more notes of caution: If you have long hair, watch so it doesn't fall into the flames when you bend over to blow out your candles; and *pay attention*—melted wax tends to splatter if you blow too forcefully.

Offerings

Offerings are small tokens of gratitude that can be placed on the altar or buried. An offering is a small gift that basically says, "Hey, higher powers, thanks for helping and protecting me!" Offerings include stones, flowers, incense, or something you've made. They should never harm or hurt anyone (and, by the way, Wiccan offerings have nothing to do with blood sacrifices . . . *yuck!*). The Goddess and God give us life, love, and daily gifts, so a simple thanks isn't too much to ask. Here is a simple prayer to say when giving an offering:

> *"Ancient deities of old,*
> *I thank thee, I thank thee.*
>
> *Goddess of many names and phases,*
> *you who protect and guide,*
> *abundance of love and fruition,*
> *hear me now and taketh thy gift,*
> *hail eternal one!*
>
> *Ancient God, father, lover, and son,*
> *you who protect and guide,*
> *solar rays of loving energies,*
> *hear me now and taketh thy gift,*
> *Hail eternal one!*
>
> *I thank thee, I thank thee.*
> *So mote it be!"*

Part Two

Enchanting:
Magickal Rules
& Circle Casting

Rules of Magick

The Wiccan Rede
"An ye harm none, do what ye will."

The Wiccan Rede is a rule that means "do no harm." When performing Magick, follow this rule strictly. Specifically, the Rede means that you are not to purposely hurt, injure, control, or abuse another. Harm none also means there should be no manipulation of another's free will. Magick is really helpful and fun! If you follow the Wiccan Rede, your spells will be successful and there will be less chance of a spell backfiring!

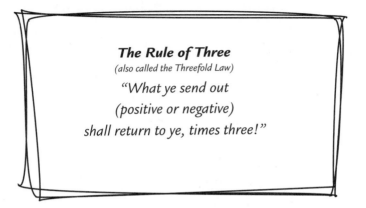

The Rule of Three
(also called the Threefold Law)

"What ye send out
(positive or negative)
shall return to ye, times three!"

This karmic rule says the actions you take and the energies you send out will eventually return threefold (three times). If you send out healing energies, you'll receive them back times three, which is a good thing! If you send out a curse or a hex for the main purpose of harming another, then you'll receive that back threefold, too.

The Wiccan Rede and the rule of three work hand in hand. These are the easiest rules to obey. If you can't follow them, you have no business being a Wiccan practitioner. Try not to worry about spells backfiring or negativity coming back to you; the chances are slim. Follow these two rules and everything will work out fine!

28

Positive versus Negative

People talk about White Witchcraft and Black Magick, but these terms are hard to decipher. How do you know what constitutes White or Black Magick? Magick itself isn't good or evil, it's the energy and intent sent by the practitioner that matters. Energy is not black or white either, but energy *can* be positive or negative. For these reasons I refer to Magick as positive or negative instead of color coding it.

Positive spells utilize good, helpful energy, and they include healing, protection, psychic awareness, and so on. Negative spells utilize hostile, harming energy. Negative energy is purposely used to harm or control another; some examples of this are curses or controlling-lust spells (I call these "zombie spells"). Negative spells go against the Wiccan Rede and have the possibility of backfiring.

To see if a spell is positive or negative, ask yourself . . .

1. Would I mind if the spell were cast on me?

2. Am I willing to take full responsibility for my actions?

3. Am I harming anyone or intruding on someone's free will?

Take your time and answer these questions each time you cast a spell. If you're still not sure whether or not you should do the spell, then don't do it! Better to be safe than sorry.

Using the Power of Magick 29

I am not going to lie to you . . . Magick spells rock! It's tempting to breeze through all this mumbo jumbo and start casting, but learning about spells first will make them more effective and prevent mistakes. To understand how important this is, keep reading!

TV, movies, and even some books portray Magick as a supernatural occurrence. The characters are born with Magick in their veins and have some funky powers; they may levitate, light candles with their minds, or freeze time. Unfortunately, none of that is real! Hollywood has tapped into the power of Witchcraft, but the unreal portrayals leave the beginner confused and wondering about the difference between fact and fiction.

Real Magick takes practice, persistence, and faith. The results are subtle but effective. Some time ago I cast a spell for a friend. He has a problem with depression and asked me to help him. First I told him that the best help he could get was from a doctor, but I agreed to do a quick spell. When I saw him a few weeks after I performed the healing spell, he told me that he had been feeling better. I know my spell didn't completely heal him,

30

but I do believe it helped him a little. Since then he has helped himself by visiting a doctor and I hear he is doing great!

One of the weirdest things about spells is that once a spell is cast, it is hard to pinpoint exactly how or when it will work. The results may be seen in a few days, weeks, or even months. This wondering comes with the territory, but after a while you get used to it and allow the Magick to work on its own, in its own time.

Visualization also plays a key role in spells. When you mentally picture an item, goal, or specific result, you are using visualization. For example, close your eyes and picture yourself finding a five-dollar bill on the sidewalk—this is visualization. Taking these creative visions and focusing on them while rubbing oil on a candle, placing herbs in a sachet, or tying knots on a cord affirms your magickal desire and sets the process in motion. Focusing on the final result instead of mentally mapping out how it will manifest allows the spell to work in its own time and way. Always remember, if you can see it, you can make it happen!

Having a realistic point of view plays an essential role in Witchcraft. For example, when performing a prosperity spell, don't expect to become a millionaire; although it isn't impossible, it's not likely. Realistic goals bring realistic results. Magick can only get you so far in life. If you want a new job, you're going to need experience in that field, and credentials. Carrying a good luck charm may provide better results than an all-out "give me the job" spell. A good luck charm will give you a boost of confidence (which would definitely help in an interview), but the job spell might prevent a more deserving person from receiving the job. Using the good luck charm is a great example of applying Magick to the mundane world. Incorporating Magick into your everyday life will help push projects along and aid in achieving your goals.

Witchcraft affects your life on the outside as much as it affects you on the inside. During our teenage years we change, grow up, and get smart. Magick has changing power, too. I believe it changed me for the better. Most importantly, I realized that with hard work and perseverance I can achieve almost anything! Don't worry, Magick can't change who you are, but it may change the way you view things. Hopefully, you'll see things in a more positive light and with a "go-get-'em" attitude!

Being a Witch means taking control of your life. The rule of three states that what you give out you get back. It also means that you and only you are responsible for your actions. It seems a little scary at first, but think about it like this: The decisions we make shape our future. So in essence we control our future. This new way of thinking has given me inner strength and courage. You, too, can experience the power of Magick, grasp control of your life, find inner strength, and achieve much-desired goals.

Out of the Broom Closet

I have heard Witchcraft referred to as the hidden magickal art. I'm sure you can understand why—the public does not exactly accept us with open arms. The main reason is that very few people understand what Wicca really is. In fact, many have never even heard of Wicca. When you decide to come out of the broom closet and tell your friends and family about your path, you will need to explain exactly what Wiccans do and why Wiccans do it.

So, what is the first step? Well, I'm glad you asked. The first step is deciding that you do indeed want to come out. Tell people you are Wiccan because you feel it is the right time, not because you feel pressure or because you feel obligated to tell people. In Wicca there are no rules about when you should come out; it is up to the individual practitioner. It could happen in a matter of weeks, months, or even years, so take your time!

If you do decide to come out, continue reading. I am sure you will find this helpful. Do actors go on stage without practicing first? No, they prepare. This is a serious issue, so you should be well prepared. Write down key points and notes about your path, and mentally prepare yourself for what you would like to say. You and I know Wicca is not an evil, devil-worshipping cult, but friends and family have no clue about what it is and what it's not. It is your job to inform them! Once you have written notes and mentally prepared yourself, it is time to take the next step.

The first person you tell should be an open-minded person whom you trust, such as a friend or a sibling. Make sure the time is right, meaning you are ready to answer questions, you are serious about this path, and you have a quiet place to talk. Try not to tell the person everything you've ever learned in one conversation, as this could overwhelm or confuse her. Your main goal is to show her that this path is positive and correct for you. Also, pay close attention to her reaction and response. Try to remember the questions she asked, because others may ask you similar questions, and you can be prepared to answer them next time.

When it comes to telling parents, I recommend it, especially if you are under eighteen. They have a right to know. I am sure they love you and hopefully they will be supportive of your path. You know them best, so you have an idea of how they will react. Review the previous steps and tell your parents the same way you told your friend or sibling—in a quiet place, with your notes, and when you are ready! After you tell them, give them time to digest all the information. You may want to leave them with reading material. Most importantly, give them time and space.

Some people won't like or respect your choice, no matter how hard you try to explain your decision to them. It's sad, but true. If a friend doesn't agree with your choice, you could agree to not talk about your path in front of him. However, if you are under eighteen and your parents or guardians ask you not to practice, then it's best to respect their decision and wait until you're older. Unfortunately, some parents just don't

34

understand. This is frustrating and disappointing. Magick will always be in your heart, and if you have to wait a few years, then you'll have to pull yourself together and have faith that in time you'll be able to practice.

Finally, the more people you tell, the easier it will become. Every day more people are beginning to see what Wicca is really about instead of clinging to bogus stereotypes. Maybe in the future Wiccans will be more accepted by others. Until then, be tolerant of other people and their faiths, and hopefully they will return the favor. Best of luck.

I Am a Witch!

So you have come out to your friends and family. Good for you. It's a hard thing to do, but you did it! Isn't it empowering? The people you chose to talk to respect you and your path (hopefully), but there are others who don't know anything about the Craft and, therefore, judge it. These people can be hostile, rude, and downright mean! Being a Witch means dealing with rubbish like this.

There are two types of nonbelievers: First, the people who make fun of the Craft, break it apart, and claim that it is fake; and second, the religious zealots who seek to save and convert you to their religious path. Both groups can bring emotional pain. The best way to handle these people is to prevent them from finding out you're a Witch. Witchcraft is a very personal path, not to mention the fact that it isn't an openly accepted faith, so keep it in a private place in your heart, and share it with close friends and family.

What do you do if someone blabs and tells the whole world? Well, hopefully it won't cause a big uproar, and it might even bring a positive light to the religion. On the other hand, the nonbelievers could have a field day. I'm telling you this to prepare you, not scare you. There aren't many books that cover this topic, and I think it's best that you know what you're getting into. The people who claim that Witchcraft isn't real or that it's silly and stupid already have proven that they are closed-minded individuals who certainly aren't speaking from experience. These unfounded opinions aren't worth listening to, so walk away and ignore such negativity.

Others believe they are trying to save your soul, which is weird because they say they care about your soul, yet they don't care about your constitutional right to freedom of religion. I was once told that I was going to hell specifically because of my faith. You could always fight back (verbally, of course), but these closed-minded people have such hard heads that nothing would get through to them, anyway. Instead, kill them with kindness and say, "You know, I am really not comfortable discussing religion with you, but thank you for your concern."

I mentioned previously that Witchcraft is a very personal path, and it is personal for many reasons. Some say you shouldn't talk about any spells you've cast because talking about them interferes with the Magick. I am not sure I believe that, but I do know that some things aren't meant to be shouted off of rooftops. And this brings me to my next point: Telling people in your school that you're a Witch for the sole purpose of intimidation or to shock them is completely disrespectful of the magickal path. If you want to come out because you don't want to keep it to yourself anymore or because you feel it will show Witchcraft in a more positive light, than more power to you, way to go! But don't come out for the wrong reasons; although the shock factor might seem like a good idea or it might be fun for a little while, eventually it will bite you in the butt!

Casting Spells for Others

Can I cast a spell for another person? you ask. You sure can, but listen up . . . there are some things you will need to know first! If a friend or family member is sick, it's natural to turn directly to a healing spell, but before you cast anything, be sure to ask the person for permission to perform a spell. There are two ways to go about asking. You can simply ask, "Hey, I want to help out. Can I cast a small healing spell for you?" Or you can be sneaky and say something like, "I am sorry you're sick. I'll send some healing energies your way," or, "I'll pray for your speedy recovery." (Please note: If you go about it this way, the sneaky way, you aren't being 100 percent truthful. Seriously consider the "harm none" aspect of the Wiccan Rede. Sometimes you want to do something good for another, but you don't necessarily want that person to find out you're a

Witch, so the "sneaky tactic" is something to ponder, but whenever possible, be honest and tell the truth!)

Whether you receive a grunt, a nod, or even a "Great, thanks!" you've got the O.K., so cast away! I know what you're thinking: *What's up with this permission thing?* Wiccans believe in free will. By casting a spell on someone without her permission (even a healing spell), you are invading on free will, which is harmful. If she doesn't want you to do a healing spell for her, then it's her loss!

On the flip side of this, you will have people approaching you asking if you'll cast a spell for them. Unfortunately, this is inevitable when you're out of the broom closet. It's up to you to decide whether or not you want to do this. What exactly is the person's motive? Is his request sincere? Does he want to control another? These are just some of the questions you should ask yourself. Remember that every spell, regardless of whom it's cast for, should harm none. Generally, healing, protection, or blessing spells are fine to cast for others. Love spells, on the other hand, are best kept to a minimum (keep reading to find out more about love spells). There is nothing wrong with helping a friend (it's even good karma), but watch out . . . once you've helped one there will surely be more to come! The last thing you want is to become a personal SpellCraft vending machine. You may want to set some limits. And finally, you may want to encourage the person to perform his own spell, or even suggest that the two of you cast it together!

38

Love Spells

"To love and be loved is to feel the sun from both sides."
David Viscott

Love spells are probably the most requested spells in Witchcraft. I guess to some degree I can understand why—genuine love can't be bought and is hard to find. Sadly, most love spells are destructive and manipulative. Yet, some aren't. So how do you know which ones are O.K. and which are not? Let's take a close look at some different types of spells.

Type A Spells

These are spells in which you control or manipulate a person into loving you. If these zombielike love spells do work, they would more than likely bring passion or lust instead of true love. Most Type A spells backfire and cause pain to both parties, or, even worse, they might actually work. Do you really want to go through a whole relationship wondering if the person likes you for you or because of the spell?

Type B Spells

These are spells you craft to manipulate the surroundings or make a specific person ask you out. Type B spells are not as harmful as Type A spells, but nonetheless, they control another person. These spells are interesting because you manipulate either the setting or a person for a short period of time. An example would be a spell you cast to work with a specific person on a school project. By working closely with this person, he will be able to see your natural charm, and maybe you will hit it off.

Type C Spells

These spells are about self-love. They are general spells to attract love or the perfect person for you at this time. Type C spells have little to no risk of backfiring because they don't control another. Self-love is really important, and such spells can be cast for healing your psyche. When you think about it, in order for any love spell to work, you have to be open to receiving love. A spell for love in general, or a spell to bring you the right person at this time, allows the higher powers to intervene and make a love connection. This type is magickally acceptable and

40

amusing! Also, make a list of your dream partner's attributes and qualities, and use this list in your spell (it certainly won't hurt!).

Love spells are complicated, but if you know what you are doing and the risk you are taking, then, by all means, cast away! You have the right to cast any spell you desire, but remember, every action has a reaction, and in Witchcraft, that reaction returns threefold.

Binding and Banishing

A binding or banishing spell can be used when a person is relentlessly picking on you (or on someone you love) and you feel threatened, either physically or emotionally, by that person's destructive behavior. Use one of these two spells when you feel someone could bring harm to himself or to another.

Positive action is hard to ignore, so combine awareness, Magick, and the protection of higher officials to gain control of the negative situation. Then the cycle can be broken and you can move on with your life.

Binding: Use to stop the direct flow of negative energy or influence in your life that is coming from a specific person, group, or situation. Also, use to halt or prevent harm and negative energy.

Banishing: Use to send a person away from you. You'll place a barrier between you and the person or situation that is threatening or harmful.

Bindings and banishings are only "Black Magick" or "negative" if you use them unwisely and in a careless manner. In certain situations they are necessary. It is best to become very familiar with them now, or you could be clueless when you desperately need the information.

What You Should Know about Binding and Banishing

1. They could backfire. Are you willing to take this risk?
2. They should be used rarely, if ever.
3. They are only used for extreme situations, so you may never need to use them.
4. You use either a binding or a banishing; both cannot be used at the same time.
5. Always cast a circle when dealing with this risky Magick.
6. Never perform a binding or banishing in the heat of the moment.
7. Be sure to follow the ensuing steps if you are going to perform a binding or banishing.

Steps to Take Before Using a Binding or Banishing Spell

If the problem you are having hasn't been resolved, then it's time to do a binding or banishing. Follow these steps strictly, and don't skip any of them.

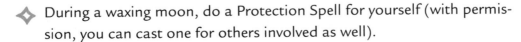

◆ During a waxing moon, do a Protection Spell for yourself (with permission, you can cast one for others involved as well).

42

✦ The next day, cut all ties with the person or people who have been causing you pain.

Wait, notice the results, then write them down.

✦ During the full or waning moon phase, send back the person's belongings and burn objects associated with him. (But keep one or two pictures of him hidden away.)

✦ During the second waxing moon phase, seal the deal with another Protection Spell (with permission, you can cast again for others who are involved).

Wait, notice the results, then write them down.

✦ If the problem persists, contact an official (if you haven't already) such as a principal, a police officer, or someone whom you believe can help protect you and your rights.

Wait, notice the results, then write them down.

✦ If the problem persists, assess the situation and think about your options. If you have no options left, once again contact officials. Then during the next waning phase, which is one or two days before the new moon (this phase is called "the dark of the moon"), do a binding or banishing.

(Note: It can help significantly if you tell one or both of your parents what's going on. They'll do everything they can to help because they love and care about you. My advise is to try your best, follow your heart, and do what's right.)

Ritual Format

About the Magick Circle

Witches perform spells and rituals in a Magick circle. This circle is a psychic barrier that aids in directing energy. The Magick circle also helps the practitioner focus, concentrate, and achieve the correct frame of mind for a ritual or spell. In a sense, it is also a source of protection, because it prevents negativity and other pesky psychic residue from entering.

(Note: Before you cast a circle, double check to make sure you have all tools [candles, herbs, cords, and so on] inside the circle.)

Define the Circle

Your circle will be mentally projected by visualization. It is erected with your energy, sweat, and power. You probably won't be able to see anything physical, but I assure you, your circle will be there, vibrating, and emanating with protective power.

44   In order to see where it begins and ends, define the circle with chalk, flowers, rocks, or a lengthy ribbon. If you use some sort of an outline, there will be less of a chance of "breaking" the circle.

The size of the circle isn't really important. As long as you have enough room to walk around, place your tools, and be comfortable, then you'll be fine.

About the Corners

The corners (also called Watchtower or Guardians) are the four directions: north, east, south, and west. These corners and their elements are invoked to keep negative energies away and oversee magickal rites.

Place a small bowl of dirt in the north of your circle. This represents that corner and sends the earthly vibration throughout the circle. You may use sand or salt in the north, incense, a bell, or a feather in the east, a red or white candle in the south, and full moon blessed water or rainwater in the west.

Some Witches use candles at each corner instead of the elemental symbols. If you choose to do this, you can use a green candle in the north, a yellow one in the east, a red one in the south, and a blue one in the west. Whichever corner representations you use, make sure you place all objects inside the circle!

North = Earth

East = Air

West = Water

South = Fire

Invocations

An invocation is a prayer or petition to the Gods and/or the corners. Invocations are performed or spoken during the Circle Casting. The invocations in the "Magick Circle Casting" (on page 49) are simple and short. You can use longer, ornate invocations from other sources, or you can use the ones you've written. (Write your own invocation on the blank page provided for you on page 47.)

Where to Cast and What to Wear

I perform my spells and rituals in my bedroom. Some Witches feel that performing rituals outside connects them with nature and the Gods, but I have no privacy in my backyard, so I would feel uncomfortable casting there. Many teens practice in their rooms. With proper lighting and some nice incense, it is actually rather pleasing.

46   When it comes to ritual garb, there are three options: (1) you can wear a robe, (2) you can wear regular clothing, or (3) you can work skyclad (in the nude).

Magickal robes can be bought or made (but you have to be crafty to make something like this). Wearing a robe is a matter of personal taste, and it tends to be more of a coven thing. I wear regular clothes during my rituals.

Performing a ritual or casting Magick has absolutely nothing to do with clothing—it is about energy, love, and inner power. Some Witches work skyclad. This is an optional practice and is up to the individual practitioner. I suggest you try a little of this and some of that until you find a style that is fitting for you.

Jewelry is also optional. When I am casting, I wear my pentacle necklace and/or my favorite onyx ring. They set the mood and give me a sense of extra protection. The Goddess and God are not picky about where you cast or what you wear, so you shouldn't be, either!

Invocation

_____

_____

_____

_____

_____

_____

_____

_____

48

Further Preparation

Before I cast my circle, I always do the following three things: I tie my hair back, take my shoes off, and turn my clock away. I happen to have big, curly hair, so I keep it up when casting in order to avoid any mishaps. I can see better that way, and I am able to sit by candles without a worry! I don't believe that shoes should be worn inside the sacred circle; it's just a matter of showing some respect, and besides, most shoes are big and bulky, so they can get in the way.

I've heard some people refer to the Magick circle as "a place between time," meaning that no time exists within your sacred space. For this reason I cover up the clock or turn it away so I cannot see the time. Watches should be taken off as well.

At times you might forget to do one or two of these three things, but try to stick to them whenever possible. I find that they can significantly affect the atmosphere within my sacred space in a positive way.

Privacy

It is important to have privacy when performing any kind of ritual. It's hard to concentrate when there are interruptions or disturbances. You can prevent these disruptions by unplugging the phone in the room you'll be using, giving the dog a bone or a toy to play with, and telling family members ahead of time that you'll need an hour to yourself!

Magick Circle Casting

Step One: Preparation

Before you cast your circle, perform the Purification Ritual provided at the end of this chapter. Although not completely necessary, it washes away negativity, mentally prepares you, and awakens the Magick within.

Step Two: Set Up

Find a quiet and private place, lay out the circle with a ribbon or cord, and place the corner/element representations in their correct places. Gather all tools and magickal supplies needed for the spell and place them inside the circle.

Step Three: Cleansing Sacred Space

There are a few different tools you can use to cleanse your sacred space. I use a ritual broom and walk clockwise, symbolically sweeping the circle and banishing unwanted energies. Also, carrying incense around the circle (clockwise) fumigates the area, thus purifying any negativity present.

Another commonly used method is to cleanse the sacred space by using saltwater. To do this, sprinkle a few grains of salt in a jar of fresh water (baby food jars work well), and mix. You may want to say a purification chant over the mixture to empower it. (See the "Purification Ritual" on page 58.) The saltwater can be used in two ways: You can either dip your first three fingers in the mixture and flick the water in a clockwise motion, or you can place fresh rosemary, mint, or sage sprigs into the saltwater and asperge (sprinkle) the circle.

50 Whichever method you use, work in a clockwise motion, visualize negativity leaving the area, and say this incantation:

*"In this place of Magick,
upon this blessed night,
from north to east and south to west,
I cleanse and purify this sacred space."*

Step Four: Centering

To center, stand in the middle of your circle and face north. Place your feet in line with your shoulders and stretch your arms up high. If you are going to use a wand to cast your circle, you may want to hold it in your power hand during this exercise. Close your eyes and take deep breaths, inhaling and exhaling slowly. Visualize your feet being part of the earth; see them as roots, an extension of you. Let your whole body become part of mother earth's energies.

Visualize a light green mist coming up from the earth, into your feet, and up through your entire body. Pull this positive loving and powerful energy into every part of your being (especially your palms). After a few moments, visualize your feet as they truly are and concentrate on your breath. Once your breathing is normal, slowly open your eyes, let your arms fall to your side, and begin to cast your circle.

Step Five: Creating a Circle of Energy

Standing before the northern corner, hold your power hand or wand out directly in line with the edge of your circle. If you are using your hand to cast the circle, you should keep your palm completely open during this process. Slowly walk clockwise (deosil) and visualize a white mist coming from your hand or wand. Allow the white mist to linger up and down, molding the circle's energy. Once you have created a circle, stop and stand in the center. Say:

"O ye ancient gods,
I cast my circle here,
in this sacred time.
Within the circle
I am protected so,
in perfect love,
in perfect trust.
This is my will.
So mote it be!"

Step Six: Invocations to the Elements / Corners
Stand before the northern corner. Point your wand or index finger to the north and say:

"Spirits of the north,
powers of earth,
come unto my circle,
I invoke thee."

Visualize a green mist coming from the north, filling you with warmth and love.

Stand before the eastern corner. Point your wand or index finger to the east and say:

> *"Spirits of the east,*
> *powers of air,*
> *come unto my circle,*
> *I invoke thee."*

Visualize air purifying you from head to toe.

Stand before the southern corner. Point your wand or index finger to the south and say:

> *"Spirits of the south,*
> *powers of fire,*
> *come unto my circle,*
> *I invoke thee."*

Visualize a barrier of fire protecting you.

Stand before the western corner. Point your wand or index finger to the west and say:

"Spirits of the west,
powers of water,
come unto my circle,
I invoke thee."

Visualize a cooling rush of water sinking into your body, cleansing you.

Step Seven: Invocations to the Goddess and God
Sit down and focus on the Goddess' energy. Light her candle (if that's the representation you used) or look at her image (a statue or picture, for example).
Say this invocation:

"Maiden, Mother, Crone,
gaining, waxing, waning,
crescent, full, and dark,
sacred dance,
sacred chants,
journey and dream,
cast down your love,
upon my sacred space,
within this sacred time,
I call to you,
growing, growing,
gaining, waxing, knowing."

54 Next, look at the image of the God (a statue or a picture) or light his candle. Focus on the Lord's energy. Say this invocation:

> *"O God, Lord of light and shadow,*
> *you who are*
> *ancient like the clouds,*
> *powerful like the lions,*
> *eternal like the Goddess;*
> *join my circle,*
> *I ask of you;*
> *come with a thousand stars,*
> *and divine solar love.*
> *Let us rejoice in Magick!"*

Step Eight: Perform the Ritual or Spell

Spells and rituals should be prepared in advance. Remember to visualize, harm none, and have fun!

Step Nine: Ground

Grounding releases extra energy into the earth. This step is necessary because it will help you feel relaxed and refreshed. Working with Magick is great fun, but sometimes you may feel anxious or tired afterward. This is when grounding exercises help. To ground, sit or lie with your palms flat out beside you and touching the floor. Visualize extra energy flowing from your palms into the ground. Concentrate on your breathing and allow any negative thoughts to travel with the flow into the earth. Finally, visualize a cool white mist coming up from the earth into your palms. Allow this light to fill you with calm and peaceful thoughts.

Step Ten: Thank the Goddess and God

If you'd like, present an offering to the Goddess and God for their help. Meditate for a few moments on their loving energies. After reflecting, it's time to bid them farewell! Whisper the following goodbye poems or, if you wish, create your own.

"Blessed be, my great Goddess,
the ritual is done,
the Magick has been cast.
Within my heart you remain,
abundant of energy you sustain.
Depart with love.
Merry meet, merry part, and merry meet again.
So mote it be!"

"Blessed be, my Lord,
the rite is over.
The spells have been conjured,
the evening is at its end.
With great love in my heart you remain,
abundant of energy you sustain.
Thank you, loving God of happiness and light.

56

> *I bid you farewell.*
> *Merry meet, merry part, and merry meet again.*
> *So mote it be!"*

Step Eleven: Release the Elements/Corners
Slowly stand up and turn toward the western corner. Point your wand or index finger to the west and say:

> *"Western spirits,*
> *element of water,*
> *I release thee*
> *with blessings and love."*

To the south,

> *"Southern spirits,*
> *element of fire,*
> *I release thee*
> *with blessings and love."*

To the east,

> *"Eastern spirits,*
> *element of air,*
> *I release thee*
> *with blessings and love."*

To the north,

> *"Northern spirits,*
> *element of earth,*
> *I release thee*
> *with blessings and love."*

Step Twelve: Open/Release Circle
Walk to the center of your circle and stand upright. In one sweeping motion, hold your wand (or hand) up and draw a small clockwise circle in the air above your head. Say:

> *"The circle is open, but unbroken,*
> *power down, to the ground."*

Point your wand or hand toward the ground, and visualize a mist falling in one quick motion to the ground.

Congratulations! You've successfully cast a circle! Clean up all the tools and relax. You may want to get something to eat or drink. Magick will make you thirsty!

58

Purification Ritual

Before rituals many Wiccans like to take a purification bath. If you have time, add purification oils and herbs to your bathwater! (See Part Four for a list of oils and herbs.) If you're like me and just don't have the time, then simply do the following before every ritual or spell.

Fill your bathroom sink with water. Add one or two drops of an essential oil (or herbs in a sachet). Stir with your index finger. Keep stirring and chant:

"In the name of the Lord and Lady,
I cleanse and purify this brew.
I stir in a clockwise motion
to enchant this Magick potion.
'Tis my witchy way,
negative energies kept at bay!"

Then rinse your face and hands. Let the water drain and, as you watch it go all the way down, send any negativity with it!

Part Three

Chants & Incantations

Magick

Throughout the first half of the book you have learned:

- ❖ The definition of Magick, which is the art of using positive energy to focus your will and create positive and useful change.

- ❖ The two magickal rules: the Wiccan Rede ("an ye harm none, do what ye will") and the Threefold Law ("what ye send out, positive or negative, shall return to ye times three").

- ❖ Magick takes practice, persistence, and faith.

- ❖ Realistic goals bring realistic results.

◆ You have the power to take control; the decisions you make shape your future.

◆ Visualization plays a key role in spells; if you can see it (mentally), you can make it happen.

Now that you know about Magick, the next half of this book will teach you how to use it. You will learn everything from writing your own spells to keeping a Book of Shadows. In other words, this is the fun part!

In this section, I've written some fun chants and incantations. (See? No need for you to worry about rhyming!) For now, you may want to breeze through them, perhaps mark the ones you like, and keep them in mind for later. In part four you'll learn how to utilize the chants and incantations, step by step, and you'll also learn about the four different types of Magick.

Chants

What is a chant? A chant is a word or phrase that is repeated over and over again. The beauty of chants is that you can use them during any spell and with almost every type of Magick! Chants are most effective when said while putting herbs in a conjuring bag, knotting a string, or lighting a candle.

Why do chants work? When you continually repeat a chant your mind slips into an altered state of consciousness. Your intention (magickal desire) connects to your brain. You're speaking your desire, hearing it, and feeling it inside.

How do you perform a chant? Close your eyes, take regular breaths, and repeat the phrase. Continue to say the chant for as long as you wish, or until you think the chant has done its work. Allow your voice to whisper and grow as it wills. Concentrate on your magickal purpose. Visualize the final outcome.

Incantations

What is an incantation? An incantation is a spell or verbal charm that is spoken. The recited formula is used to produce a specific magickal effect. An incantation doesn't have to rhyme (but many chants do). When spoken, the words have a powerful and deep magickal tone to them. How do you use an incantation? Say the incantation once, in a serious voice, while visualizing your magickal need strongly. Incantations may work on their own, but they are more powerful when utilized with candles, conjuring bags, and so on.

In the following pages there are several chants and incantations to use for various purposes. Under some of the chants and incantations are "notes." These notes are ideas and suggestions. You don't have to follow them, but they have been included for your benefit to help you along.

Chants and Incantations

64

Banishing

Banishing
(Incantation)
I banish thee
he's (she's) filled with
harm and evil you see
I banish thee forever from me
and any harm from thee to me
shall dissipate by
my count of three
one—I sever the ties
two—I'm through with you
three—I'm set free
so mote it be!

Banishing
(Incantation)
On the night of Magick's peak
with good intentions I now speak
———— has done great harm
I wish not to curse
but to let ————'s anger disperse
I banish this hurt
I banish this pain
I banish the person with this name
I wish him (her) peace
I wish him (her) wellness
but I wish him (her) gone
banish this evilness!

Banish Evil
(Chant)
Midnight flame, midnight flame
banish thy evil
and undo this pain.

Blessing

Blessings Upon It
(Incantation)

Air, earth, spirit, and fire
I present to you my magickal desire
oceans and seas, waters of purification
I speak this rhyming incantation
blessings upon _____
I cast positive energies through thee
with harm to none
my will be done
so mote it be!

(Note: Because this incantation
mentions water, you may want to
incorporate it into your spell.)

A Tool Blessing
(Incantation)

Bless this new _____
may the positive power endure
forever more
strengthen and empower
during this bewitching hour,
negativity kept at bay
I bless this tool
in every way.

Blessing
(Chant)

Powers above
and below,
sun and sea,
bless this _____
so mote it be!

(Note: This chant works
really well for a tool blessing.)

66

Binding

Poppet Binding
(Incantation)

Let the words be rhyming
spoken with magickal timing
darkest ribbon black
I now weave front to back
poppet to man
one and the same
thou art one
weaving winding
binding binding
now you naught harm
your evil power is gone
by this spoken charm!

(Note: Use a black ribbon
to bind a poppet.)

Binding
(Chant)

Weaving, winding, binding, binding
weaving, winding, binding, binding.

A Funky Binding

(Incantation)

Sweet and slow
toe to foe
ounce and pounce
pickle and bubble
stop your pain
stop your game
thrice about the karma sends out
bound and bind
I made up my mind
this will stop you here
in your tracks dear
you'll harm none
and that means no one
so mote it be!

Bind

(Incantation)

By shining moon and sea
I place a bind upon his (her) name
so neither his (her) actions
nor words bring pain!

68

Book Blessing

Book Blessing
(Incantation)

Beautiful Goddess in all your phases
protect and bless these magickal pages
from spills and ills
and evil spirits
conjure and charm
all near it!

Grimoire Blessing
(Incantation)

All powers positive and divine
bless this Grimoire of mine
seal it with the Witches' sign
may none harm it
in any way or any time.

(Note: The Witches' sign is a pentacle—
a five-pointed star with a circle around it.
Visualize the pentacle over the Grimoire.)

Magickal Book
(Incantation)

Protect my writings in this magickal book
no evil nor negative people may look
as I seal it with positive energy
may it be charmed times three!

Witch's Book

(chant)

Witches' secrets that you keep
shall be protected as I speak
naught evil nor fire shall reach
enhance thy pages and the lessons they teach
bless this book with divine power
during the bewitching hour.

Healing

Healing Flame
(Incantation)

By my will, by my might
by this candle bright
sickness burn in the flame
it cannot hurt or maim
healing power now take flight
I conjure wellness tonight
by my will
by my might
I cast this spell and make it right!

(Note: You may want to use
a candle with this incantation.)

Healing
(Chant)

Past and time

hear my rhyme

heal me, cure me

illness be gone

kept at bay

away, away.

(Note: "Me" can be changed to "he"
or "she" if the spell is for another.)

To Keep a Witch Well
(Incantation)

To keep a Witch well

cast this funky spell

a little of this and some of that

sprinkle deosil

a tit a tat

mix a mat

double wink

triple blink

potions brew

health will do

keep the cold away

and that nasty flu at bay

in good health

yup, that's me

so mote it be!

Healing Power
(Chant)

Magick, Magick, mend and fix

heal this sickness

send to me your healing power

on this and every hour.

Love

Love
(Incantation)

Hear my will
I wish for love
come to me
craft it be
by the powers above and below
love come to me
so mote it be!

Love Within
(Chant)

Beltis, Branwen, Hathor, and Diana
Goddesses of love
hear my plea,
I seek love within me!

Red Means Love
(Incantation)

Brew this witchy potion
to evoke this notion
blood red candles
burn with fire
I enchant his desire
lust and love
magick ride true
up in the air I send for you!

To Summon a Prince
(Chant)

Silver moon, shining bright
send to me my Mr. Right
mugwort, yarrow, and some mints
banish the toad and summon my prince!

Lover's Passion
(Incantation)

Raging fire of desire,
ignite his (her) passion,
in an uncontrolling fashion.

(Note: Because it says "raging fire,"
you may want to incorporate
a candle into your spell.)

74

Beauty

Beauty
(Incantation)

Elements of four please aid me in my task
I seek beauty that will last
this is what others see
here is what I wish to be
work as I will, work as I must
I cast my Magick in perfect love
and perfect trust
one, two, three, I conjure thee
I have spoken my will
so mote it be!

(Note: Present a picture or a drawing,
or strongly visualize "what you wish to be.")

Bewitching Beauty
(Chant)

Bewitch and conjure
beauty be mine
in the nick of time
beauty now shine
with thy rhyme.

Beauty
(Chant)

Beautiful as a swan,
imperfections now be gone!

Beauty Charm

(Incantation)

Let me shine like a star
conjure close, conjure far
facade they see, change for me
enchant and charm
cause no harm
flower pink, beauty spell
work your best and work well!

(Note: You may want to incorporate
a pink flower into the spell.)

Money

Banish Debt

(Incantation)

I banish my debt

I have needs that must be met

release the hold and open the way

so money may flow my way every day!

Money
(Chant)

Money, money
come my way
with growth and gain;
by my might,
the time
is right!

Prosperity
(Chant)

Prosperity green
prosperity green
I open my hand
now come to me
hear my plea
prosperity green!

Abundance
(Incantation)

Abundance of money come today
into my life grow and stay
debt be gone, far away
forever now kept at bay.

78

Truth

Lunae Lumen: Truth

(Chant)

Lunae lumen

lunae lumen

hear my plea

send me the truth

so I may see.

(Note: "Lunae lumen" is Latin for "moonbeam."
It's best to do this chant
at night and in view of the moon.)

Unveil the Mysteries

(Chant)

Within the light
that burns so bright
unveil the mysteries I seek tonight.

(Note: Because this chant mentions
"light" and "burn," you may want
to incorporate a candle.)

Truth to See

(Incantation)

Ancient ones,
I cast this spell,
for clarity and truth to see,
show what's unknown to me!

80

STOP GOSSIP

Death to Gossip
(Incantation)

Mind your business

do not pry

words of hatred and evilness die

move on and leave me be

let the gossip

float to sea

bad things done and said

leave my life

be gone and dead.

A Secret
(Chant)

Keep this secret

close to heart

from your lips

it shall not part!

Gossip Stop
(Incantation)

Gossip stop by my count of three
truth be mine, let them see
one—gossip be done
two—it is through
three—now let them see!

Stop Gossip
(Chant)

Mouths that chatter wickedness
I seal your lips against this evilness
speak not ill of me
I cast my will
so mote it be!

Karma
(Incantation)

Karma wheel turns thrice about
nix those evil words you shout
whispers bane and giggles hate
seal you now a threefold fate!

82

Purification

Cleanse Thee
(Chant)

East, west, water brew
full moon cast, shadow dew
purify and cleanse thee
as I will, so shall it be.

Purification
(Incantation)

In this night and in this hour
I call upon the Ancient Power
to cleanse and purify _____
as north is to earth, south is to fire
bring to me my magickal desire
east o' the sun, west o' the moon
_____ is purified by the
Witches' Rune.

(Note: The Witches' Rune is the pentacle.)

Cleanse and Purify
(Chant)

Silver light throughout and about
earth, air, moon, and sun
all evil stay out
by the power of one
I cleanse and purify
as I will
so it be done!

(Note: Visualize a silver light cleansing.)

power

Power
(Incantation)

One for the spell
two I cast it well
three I make it be
four make it sure
five points to the star
six near or far
seven cast the circle here
eight last for weeks straight
nine the power is mine!

(Note: This works great with
knot Magick or nine herbs.)

Enchanting Power
(chant)

Say these words to enchant
nothing shall reverse or recant
power increase threefold good
power grow like you should.

Increase Power
(Incantation)

Hubble, bubble, cause no trouble
power increase, power double
four winds, fate, and magickal power
gain now with every hour.

84

Protection

Protection in Every Way

(Incantation)

Earth and sea
keep harm from me
evil turn away
by night
by day
I am protected
in every way!

Protection from thy Enemy

(Incantation)

Words of the flickering flame
take this offering
hear my plea
tame thy enemy,
injustice has been done
I seek your protection from this evil one!

(Note: Place an offering [such as a flower or incense] before you as you recite the words "take this offering.")

Protection Charm
(Incantation)

Say this spoken charm
to prevent harm
five-point star and circle round
protects from sky to ground
conjure a silver light when the time is right
let it surround you in the mist so bright
and protected ye will be day and night!

(Note: Visualize a silver mist
surrounding you in a circle.)

Beneath the Moon
(Incantation)

Beneath the moon I pray tonight
to the Moon Goddess shining bright
halt the harm and turn it away
evil intentions kept at bay
raise a shield of protection and light
so none can harm, day or night.

86

PSYCHIC POWERS

Psychic/Divination
(Incantation)

Heed and hinder
hear the Witches' call
left or right
silly or trite
may the candles glow tonight
let the knowledge flow
and show me all I wish to know!

(Note: This can be used to open psychic
abilities or when you perform divination.)

Sight
(Chant)

Mystical veil that clouds my sight
dissipate upon this night.

Psychic
(Incantation)

Upon this night the witching hour
I seek the psychic power
amethyst, amber, and more
let the strength endure
psychic sight flow
show me all I wish to know!

Premonition
(Chant)

Stone, earth, and fire
bring my desire
enhance my vision
with the power of premonition.

Psychic Power
(Chant)

Third eye ready, nice and steady
psychic power grow stronger
ignorant I am no longer!

An Undoing Spell

Words of Wisdom: A Poem

To undo a spell
you think didn't go well

Listen and learn
a spell shouldn't turn

I hope you didn't forget
the rule of three I did threat

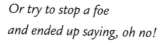

Maybe something went funny
did you ask for too much money?

Or try to stop a foe
and ended up saying, oh no!

This charm may help
but a lesson you have learned
and the Rule of Three
may once again return!

The Spell

(Note: Every action has a reaction. Most controlling love spells backfire, and some money spells get out of control. Every once in awhile a mistake happens and the spell just doesn't work. This undoing spell might help, but you have to take responsibility for what you've done.)

You will need one black candle and a pin.

Cast your Magick circle. Bless the black candle.

On the candle, carve the words "Undo it," as well as the name of the spell, the person for whom it was cast, and the date it was performed. Light the candle and say this incantation:

"Undo it, undo it
once, twice, through it
I take the power back
by this candle black
undo it, undo it
once, twice, through it
by the power of one
it's undone!"

As soon as possible, bury or burn all the cords, herbs, or ciated with the spell you are "undoing." Make sure th the way down.

Part Four

Bewitching:
Correspondences
& Magickal Properties

How to Write Your Own Spells

In order to write any spell, you must first decide on your magickal desire. What exactly do you want to accomplish? Stick to one goal at a time; you will always have the option of writing new spells at a later date.

When I first started writing my own spells, I studied some that I had gotten off the Internet and from books. After I looked at them in depth, I noticed a pattern. Each spell had a list of ingredients (herbs or incense, for example), a certain type of Magick (such as candle Magick or conjuring bags), a chant or incantation, and a suggested a course of action (like rubbing oils on a candle).

In order to write a spell you'll need to know proper correspondences. Correspondences are magickal properties of certain herbs, colors, incense, oils, and so on. When you smell eucalyptus oil or herb, you may think of healing. This means eucalyptus and healing correspond with each other. To make things easier for you, in this book I have included correspondences of charms, herbs, and colors for each magickal purpose.

I could have written a spell book that included full spells; however, that is not the point I am trying to make. I think all Witches should know how to write their own spells. On the following page you will find "Eleven Magickal Steps to Writing and Casting a Bewitching Spell." This outline is the foundation that my system stands upon. It pulls all the elements of a spell together, making things a lot simpler.

If a particular spell you desire is not covered in this book, by using this system and doing some research (finding proper correspondences), you will be able to create a spell from scratch.

Eleven Magickal Steps to Writing and Casting a Bewitching Spell

Prepare

1. Pick out a chant for your magickal purpose. Create a list of what you will need for this spell.

2. Figure out the best moon phase.

3. Choose the type of Magick that will work best with your particular need.

4. Select a color theme.

5. Depending on your type of Magick, gather the proper tools. (For example, if you are working with candle Magick, you will need an appropriately colored candle. If you are working with conjuring bags, you will need the proper herbs, and so on.)

Casting

1. Bring all tools and magickal items you are going to use into your circle.

2. Check the list to see if you have everything.

3. Cast the circle.

4. Perform the action, visualize, and say the chant or incantation.

5. Close the circle.

6. Record your experience.

Sample Spell

Spell Created: May 24

Spell Brewed: May 27

Money Conjuring Bag

Magickal Checklist

Type of Magick: conjuring bag

Color Theme: green and silver

Herbs: sage, cinnamon, and basil

Charms: three dimes

Tools: wand, Book of Shadows

Best Moon Phase: waxing or full moon

For Whom/Reason: for me, to bring more money into my life

Materials Needed: green fabric, silver tie, and ribbon

The Spell: I cast the Magick circle and lay the green cloth flat out in front of me. Then I sprinkled the herbs (one tablespoon of each) in the center and dropped in the three dimes, placed my hands over the mixture, and visualized money coming into my life. I said the following chant three times:

"Money, money,
come my way;
with growth and gain,
by my might,
the time is right!"

I then pulled the edges of the cloth up and tied with the silver ribbon, and grounded and closed the circle. I will now record all information in my Book of Shadows. It is done!

Additional Notes: The spell was easy to write and cast. It took approximately forty-five minutes to cast the spell, from beginning to end. I need to work on visualization techniques.

Results Seen: Results were seen mid-June. I received a twenty-dollar refund in the mail and I might get a new job.

Moon Phases:
When to Cast Your Spells

The moon phases have been followed for hundreds of years. Farmers planted seeds during the new or waxing phase so the moon's vibration aided in the seeds' growth. For this very reason, Witches cast specific spells during certain moon phases. Working with the moon's phases may seem complicated at first, but it isn't!

To figure out which phase the moon is in you may want to check out *The Old Farmer's Almanac* or *Llewellyn's Magical Almanac,* or read the weather section of a current newspaper. The moon's cycle is twenty-eight days long and begins with the new moon, which is when little or no moon is visible. Over a period of days it grows, increasing in size; this phase is called waxing. The moon waxes until we are able to see the moon in its entirety (full moon). The bright full moon then decreases (waning) into the new moon once again. This cycle has been repeating itself for centuries.

You may have noticed that I didn't mention the quarter or crescent moons; this is because Witches lean toward simplicity and generally work only with the four main phases. There is another moon phase called the dark of the moon. It appears one or two days before the new moon. But, as you read on, you'll see that Witches rarely work with the dark of the moon.

What follows is a list of the moon's phases. You will learn about the types of spells that can be cast during each phase and the best time to tap into each phase's power.

New Moon

This is when no crescent or only the smallest crescent is visible. Magickally, the new moon is a great time to start new projects and plant seeds for later growth. The vibration of the new moon yields new beginnings and a fresh outlook. The new moon's energy can be tapped into the night before, the night of, and the night after the new moon.

Types of spells cast on the new moon: spells for blessing, money, or new ventures.

98

Waxing Moon

This is when the moon grows. Magickally, the waxing moon allows us to increase something or draw in positive energies. The vibration of the waxing moon signifies growth and expansion. The waxing moon's energy can be utilized the second day after the new moon to the second day before the full moon.

Types of spells cast during the waxing moon: spells for love, beauty, money, protection, or health and healing.

Full Moon

This is when the moon is completely round and visible. Magickally, the moon is at its highest power. The vibration of the full moon adds an extra oomph to all spells. The energy flows the night before, the night of, and the night after the full moon, so tap into the moon's energy at these times.

Types of spells cast during the full moon: spells for psychic power, truth, to stop gossip, or to increase power.

Waning Moon

This is when the moon decreases in size. Magickally, the waning moon releases, banishes, or makes something smaller. The vibration of the waning moon allows us to let go of negative energy and cleanse the soul. The best time to tap into its energy is the second day after the full moon to the second day before the new moon.

Types of spells cast during the waning moon: spells for cleansing, purification, banishing, binding, or to stop gossip.

Dark of the Moon

This is when no moon is visible. Magickally, the dark of the moon banishes unwanted energies. This is a time for rest and contemplation. The dark of the moon doesn't last long; it releases its power only one or two days before the new moon, so tap into its energy at this time.

Types of spells cast during the dark of the moon: spells for bindings and banishings.

If you desperately need to cast a particular spell, but it isn't the right moon phase, you can alter the spell to fit the current phase. For example, a spell to increase money can be cast during the new, waxing, or full moon phase. Or if the current phase is waning, you can alter the spell a bit so it banishes debt.

For more advanced magickal timing, look into astrological phases, planetary hours, quarter moons, and days of the week.

Types of Magick

There are a bunch of ways to cast a spell. You can use candles, conjuring bags, poppets, knots, and so on. These tools used in conjunction with visualization and the spoken word can bring about the desired magickal result, goal, or purpose.

If you're just beginning to work with Magick, you should keep the spells simple. Eventually you may want to experiment and combine

100

several types of Magick. Mixing and matching types of Magick can add extra energy to spells. On the following pages you will learn about candle Magick, conjuring bags, knot Magick, and poppets. Please note that these are just examples of the many types of Magick that exist.

Candle Magick

Candle Magick utilizes the element of fire to produce bewitching results! To use candle Magick you will need the following: a candle of the correct color (see "Magickal Colors," page 105), a specific herb or oil that corresponds with your magickal desire, a small sheet of paper, a pen, and a sturdy candle holder.

Step One: Cast a circle if you would like to. Make sure you have all the ingredients ready. You will also need a lighter or matches to light the candle, and a damp paper towel (herbs and oils are sticky).

Step Two: Hold the candle in your power hand (the one you write with) and visualize a white light coming from your hand into the candle, charging it with your magickal desire.

Step Three: Apply the herb or essential oil to the candle and visualize the final outcome. Rub in a clockwise motion to increase, bring, or build. Rub counterclockwise to banish or decrease.

Step Four: On a piece of paper, write your magickal purpose and place it under the candle. Put the candle in the holder, light it, and say the chant or incantation.

Conjuring Bags

Conjuring bags (also called herbal sachets or mojo bags) used in conjunction with a chant or incantation create a specific magickal effect. To make a conjuring bag you will need the following items: scissors, fabric or cloth of the correct color (see "Magickal Colors," page 105), ribbon (color specific), and herbs and charms that match your magickal desire.

Step One: Cast a circle if you desire. Make sure you have all the ingredients ready. Cut the fabric or cloth into a circular shape. The size should be between five and nine inches in diameter.

Step Two: Sprinkle one tablespoon of each herb in the center of the cloth, then drop a charm into the mixture.

Step Three: Place your hands over the mixture and visualize your goal strongly. Say the chant or incantation.

Step Four: Pull up the edges (while leaving the herbs and charms in the center) and tie with the ribbon to close.

(Note: If you don't have fabric, you can use an envelope of the correct color and place the herbs and charms inside.)

Knot Magick

Knot Magick is simple and effective. As you concentrate on tying the knots, you maintain your focus, thus pulling all your attention into this task. You'll need a piece of paper, a pen, and embroidery floss or satin cord (called *rattail*) of an appropriate color (see "Magickal Colors," page 105). The floss or cord should be either ten or twenty-four inches long.

To begin, cast your circle. Take a few minutes to figure out exactly what your need is, then write it down or draw a picture of it. Close your eyes and see it in your mind as clearly as you can. Hold the ends of the string/cord taut and infuse your energy into it, visualizing your desire.

Tie a knot in the center, concentrating on your desire. Start saying the chant or incantation (select a chant or incantation that is best suited for your magickal desire). Continue tying the knots in this order:

When it's finished, seal it with a kiss. Leave it on your dresser, wear it, or bury it. Don't undo the knots unless you wish to undo the spell.

Poppet Magick

You may think poppets are used to hex or curse someone, but in Wiccan Magick they are used to bring about positive results. Use poppets to heal, to stop gossip, or for love, binding, or even money. Throw out your old way of thinking; poppets, if used in the proper way, have the potential to work and reap extraordinary results.

In Magick there is a law of similarity. This law essentially states that what you do to the symbolic representation of a person, thing, or situation will have some sort of an effect on the person, thing, or situation. Combining a specific charm (a picture of the person, a handwriting sample, and so on) with visualization and knowledge of the law of similarity produces effective Magick. Remember, Magick poppets should never be used to harm, hurt, control, or injure another.

To make a poppet you will need a small charm to empower the doll. If the spell pertains to a person, it could be an item belonging to that person, a handwriting sample, or a picture. If the spell is for a situation or thing (such as to stop gossip), then write on a red piece of paper "Stop Gossip." For money matters, on a green sheet of paper write "Prosperity," and fold the paper around three dimes. Make sure you have decided on a certain charm before you start the spell.

Creating the Doll

Using a sheet of paper, trace the poppet pattern provided for you in the appendix (page 138), then cut it out. This will be the pattern. Get some fabric (make sure it is the correct color for your magickal purpose); an old shirt, a cotton handkerchief, or felt can also be used. Trace the image onto the fabric using the pattern. Cut out two identical shapes and place one on top of the other.

(Note: For a bigger doll, make the pattern larger.)

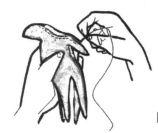

Sewing the Doll

Take a needle and thread, and slowly sew the two shapes together. On one of the legs, leave two inches unsewn. Using this hole, turn the poppet inside out.

Stuffing the Doll

Stuff the doll with fluff, cotton balls, white yarn, or Spanish moss. You may want to use herbs matching your magickal purpose. Put the charm in the poppet and sew it up. Say the chant or incantation and visualize your magickal goal strongly.

(Note: For a binding or stop gossip spell you may want to wrap a black ribbon around the doll while saying the chant.)

Caring for Your Poppet After the Spell

Once the spell is completed, you will need a safe place to keep the poppet. You may want to leave it on your altar to continuously intensify the power. If you are unable to keep the poppet on an altar, tuck it away somewhere safe, like in a drawer or a shoebox. After three months, hold the poppet in your hands and say this incantation:

"Three months ago, on a bewitching (day of the week) night,
I cast a spell to make things right.
The desired results have come.
I seal the spell
so it naught be undone."

Visualize a pentacle on the poppet and continue the incantation by saying:

"Unless it does harm,
let this poppet continue to charm.
As I will, so mote it be."

You may bury the poppet in a safe and secure place, or keep it where you had it before. You will feel the effects of the spell for a few months. If for some reason the spell backfires or you wish to undo the spell, do not perform the previous ritual. Instead, search through Part Three, Chants & Incantations, and locate the undoing spell. Perform it within your protective circle.

Magickal Colors

Protection: green, white, red, blue, silver, black, brown (for pets).

Purification: white, light blue, silver, black (for banishing unwanted energies).

Healing and health: green, white, red, blue, purple (for mental aspects).

106

Blessing: white, light yellow, silver, green (for mother earth), light blue.

Book blessing: white, silver, light yellow, purple.

Money: green, silver, gold, white (use with green or silver), red (mainly for success).

Love: pink (for sweet love), red (for passionate love, sexuality, and lust), white (use with red or pink), purple (spiritual love).

Truth: white, yellow, silver, green (for wisdom), dark blue (for justice and legal matters).

Banishing: black, dark red.

Binding: black, white (for a more gentle effect).

Stop gossip: red, black, dark green (use with black).

Power: red, bright blue, orange (for vitality).

Beauty: pink, yellow (confidence and charm), red (courage and attraction), purple (for femininity).

Psychic powers: purple, white (for wisdom), green (for divination work), dark blue (for intuition).

Herbs and Charms

Using Herbs and Charms

Herbs are commonly used in conjuring bags, but they can be used for all types of Magick! They can also be rubbed (or sprinkled) around a candle, used in loose incense mixtures and in dream pillows, and stuffed in poppets. Most herbs used in Magick are kitchen herbs, meaning they can be found in almost any kitchen cabinet. So check your cabinets—you may be surprised at what you find.

Herbs and flowers hold vibrant magickal energy because they are mother earth's gifts.

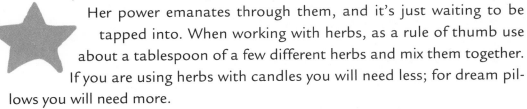

Her power emanates through them, and it's just waiting to be tapped into. When working with herbs, as a rule of thumb use about a tablespoon of a few different herbs and mix them together. If you are using herbs with candles you will need less; for dream pillows you will need more.

There are so many herbs available, but I will only list a few that are commonly used. If you enjoy working with herbs, look into a few books on this topic.

Charms are small trinkets such as crystals, shells, or coins that can be utilized in Magick. Almost anything can become a charm.

Over the next few pages I have listed some herbs and charms (and stones that can be utilized as charms) for each magickal purpose. Feel free to add your own items to the list of charms.

1◉8

Protection

Herbs: basil, bay Leaf, chamomile, cinnamon, garlic, rosemary, black pepper, clove, juniper, fennel, pine, peppermint, parsley, spanish moss, lavender, sage, vervain, sandalwood, lilac, angelica, burdock, carnation, dill, ginseng, horehound, hyssop, mugwort, nettle, orris, pennyroyal, valerian, vetivert, willow, witch hazel, wormwood, comfrey, ivy, rue, slippery elm, yarrow, patchouli.

Charms: safety pin, small mirror, horseshoe symbol, moon symbols, bell, pentacle, sea salt or regular salt, photo and/or writing sample of the person in need of protection. *The following stones can be utilized as protection charms:* agate, beryl, citrine, diamond, garnet, jade, jasper, lapis lazuli, lepidolite, malachite, moonstone, onyx, peridot, sapphire, sun stone, tiger's-eye, topaz, tourmaline, turquoise.

Purification

Herbs: dill, eucalyptus, juniper, pine, basil, bay leaf, garlic, lemon grass, all citrus rinds, sage, vervain, hyssop, parsley, valerian, ginger, lemon balm, lavender, lilac, sandalwood.

Charms: pentacle, full moon blessed water, sea salt or regular salt, soap shreds, feather. *The following stones can be utilized as purification charms:* aquamarine, calcite, garnet, quartz, lapis lazuli.

Healing

Herbs: pine, carnation, rosemary, gardenia, angelica, chamomile, garlic, horehound, bay leaf, nettle, rue, sage, mugwort, vervain, burdock, ginseng, juniper, violet, willow, eucalyptus, lavender, thyme, sandalwood, clove, mints, basil, oregano.

Charms: four-leaf clover, horseshoe symbol, dirt, red yarn, shells with hole, seashells, cork, moon symbols, photo and/or writing sample of the person in need of healing. *The following stones can be utilized as healing charms:* aventurine, azurite, beryl, bloodstone, celestite, garnet, hematite, jade, jasper, lapis lazuli, rose quartz, smoky quartz, sodalite, sunstone, topaz, turquoise, zircon.

Blessings and Book Blessings

Herbs: marigold, rosemary, sage, pine, frankincense, sandalwood, dragon's blood, dill, basil.

Charms: pentacle, moon symbols, full moon blessed water, seasalt or regular salt, bell. *The following stones can be utilized as blessing charms:* clear quartz, onyx, moonstone, as well as all protection, purification, and power stones.

Money

Herbs: basil, nutmeg, sage, patchouli, ginger, lemon, cinnamon, dill, mints, sesame seeds, allspice, pine, vetivert, chamomile, fenugreek, vervain, jasmine, orange.

11⊕

Charms: dimes, silver coins, four-leaf clover, money symbols. *The following stones can be utilized as money charms:* aventurine, bloodstone, calcite, opal, emerald, jade, lapis lazuli, malachite, peridot, tiger's-eye, topaz, tourmaline, turquoise, jasper, pyrite.

Love

Herbs: roses, ginger, lemon and orange rinds, yarrow, rosemary, vanilla, cardamon, all pink and red flowers, basil, marjoram, chamomile, jasmine, daisy, lavender, mints, thyme, clove, catnip, cinnamon, patchouli, vetivert, gardenia, ivy, pennyroyal, vervain, juniper, orris, rue, valerian, violet, willow, wormwood.

Charms: pennies, copper, rings, acorns, pinecones, rice, feather, heart symbols, seashells, shells with holes, sea salt or regular salt, morning dew. *The following stones can be utilized as love charms:* agate, amethyst, beryl, emerald, jade, lapis lazuli, malachite, moonstone, ruby, rose quartz, rhodochrosite, sapphire, topaz, tourmaline.

Truth

Herbs: sandalwood, basil, sage, slippery elm, bay leaf, marigold, sunflower.

Charms: moon symbols, sand, feather, cork, flour, symbols of justice. *The following stones can be utilized as truth charms:* malachite, rhodonite, sodalite, tiger's-eye, clear quartz, jade, sapphire.

Banishing

Herbs: elderberries, frankincense, horehound, juniper, nettle, pine, solomon's seal, lemon rind, garlic, black pepper, sandalwood.

Charms: bells, sea salt or regular salt, black or red ribbon, photo of the person you wish to banish and/or a writing sample from that person. *The following stones can be utilized as banishing charms:* obsidian, clear quartz, malachite, onyx.

Binding

Herbs: nettle, garlic, patchouli, frankincense, vines, thyme, dragon's blood. (Note: The best combination is nettle, garlic, and one pinch of dragon's blood.)

Charms: safety pin, rubber band, dirt, sea salt or regular salt, black ribbon, photo of the person you wish to bind and/or a writing sample from that person. *The following stones can be utilized as binding charms:* onyx, clear quartz, topaz.

Stop Gossip

Herbs: clove, myrtle, eucalyptus, slippery elm.

Charms: safety pin, small mirror, pentacle, cork. *The following stones can be utilized as stop-gossip charms:* carnelian, ruby, opal, smoky quartz, topaz.

Power

Herbs: dragon's blood, ginger, citrus rinds, black pepper, carnation, mugwort, pennyroyal, bay, pine, vanilla, nutmeg, cinnamon.

Charms: pentacle, dirt, moon and sun symbols, red ribbon. *The following stones can be utilized as power charms:* ruby, agate, beryl, bloodstone, garnet, jasper, malachite, onyx, opal, rhodochrosite, tiger's-eye, tourmaline.

Beauty

Herbs: catnip, rose, ginseng, vervain, lilac, marjoram, rosemary, yarrow, daisy, baby's breath, lavender.

Charms: small mirror, rice, morning dew, seashells, feather, pink sparkles, photo of the person for whom this spell is directed and/or a writing sample from that person. *The following stones can be utilized as beauty charms:* jasper, moonstone, opal, rose quartz, zircon, amber, rhodochrosite.

Psychic Powers

Herbs: angelica, mugwort, yarrow, rose, star anise, galangal, jasmine, thyme, chamomile, bay, cinnamon, lemon grass, nutmeg, sandalwood.

Charms: pentacle, purple ribbon, moon symbols, silver coins, full moon blessed water. *The following stones can be utilized as psychic power charms:* amethyst, aquamarine, azurite, beryl, citrine, lapis lazuli, lepidolite, moonstone, topaz.

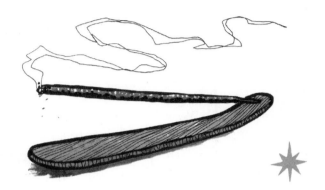

Incense

When I first became a Wiccan, I didn't really know about incense. I remember my mother and me standing in the kitchen with an incense stick reading the directions on the package. How do I light this thing? What will it smell like?

After some time I grew used to the comforting scents, and I started building a collection. I use incense a lot. Scent is a powerful calming agent. When I cast my circle I place an incense stick in the east and one in the north, where I usually do my spell work.

There are three types of incense: stick, cone, and loose. An incense stick is about twelve inches long. One end of the stick is wood, and this end is placed in an incense holder. To light an incense stick, hold the wooden part and light the tip. Blow out the flame. You will see an orange-red glowing ember at the tip. The smoke that you'll see is the smoldering fragrance.

114

A cone incense is about two inches high. To light a cone incense, grasp the widest part with your fingers and carefully light the small tip. Blow out the flame quickly. Place the cone incense in an incense holder and watch for the ember and smoke. Sometimes cone incense is tricky to light, and may take several attempts.

Loose incense is a combination of herbs and resins that is placed on a charcoal disk. Loose incense is usually mixed prior to a ritual. This type is the hardest to use. Try working with sticks and cones first, and gradually make your way to loose incense and charcoals. To use loose incense, research some good recipes for your particular purpose. During the correct moon phase create the mixture and store it in a jar until you are ready to use it. For this type of incense I strongly suggest you light it in front of a parent, then carefully bring it into your circle, which should already be laid out.

Using tweezers or tongs, hold the charcoal and light the end with a candle flame. These are special charcoals that come from New Age or metaphysical stores. (Do not use barbeque charcoals.) The charcoal will spark, so try not to put your face too close to the charcoal. When the end starts to burn and you see a gray-white ash, carefully place the charcoal down in a fireproof container (something made of cast iron). Wait about four minutes until the ash comes over the top of the incense disk. Sprinkle one tablespoon of the loose mixture onto the charcoal. Add more incense to the coal every five minutes.

This type of incense is rather complicated to use, and, to be honest with you, incense is incense; for the most part, all methods will produce the same smell. One time I was performing a Yule ritual, and I placed a charcoal disk in my new glass ashtray. I figured that because it was an ashtray it would be heat resistant, but toward the end of my ritual it broke in half. The noise almost scared me to death. I quickly called my mother and she poured a glass of water on the mixture. Luckily, nobody was hurt, and nothing was burned. Due to this experience, I rarely use loose incense and charcoals. If you do choose to utilize this type of incense, be careful and always remain alert.

Magickal Oils

Oil blends are often used in aromatherapy. Traditional aromatherapy users say that if placed on the pulse points (your wrists) or simmered in an oil burner, specific oil scents can bring about tranquility, peace, and happiness. In Magick, special oil blends are used to anoint candles, the body, and charms and amulets. This oil then sends surges of power through the candle, person, or charm. To create a magickal oil, fragrance oils and essential oils are mixed together, then added to a base oil.

Fragrance oils are synthetic, meaning manmade, and essential oils are the extract of plants, flowers, and herbs. Some Witches prefer to work only with essential oils because they come directly from nature, but fragrance oils come in a wider array of scents and can cost about half of what essential oils cost. Because of this, I find it best to work with a little of this and some of that!

Both oils are very potent and strong, so diluting them before use is necessary. This is where a "base oil" comes in handy. The base oil helps weaken the fragrance oils and essential oils so the mixture smells better and won't irritate your skin if applied. Blending a base oil of grape seed, olive oil, or sesame oil with the essential oil or fragrance oil creates a safe, magickal mixture. On page 118 you'll find more information on how to properly mix your magickal oils.

Tools

To conjure up a magickal oil, you'll need a few tools. Most of these tools can be found around the house, in craft stores, or in hardware shops. To start you'll need an eyedropper, a small funnel, and a few empty jars (preferably with caps). Baby food jars work well, but I found that they are a bit big; however, if you fill them less than half full, you'll be able to stretch your supplies further!

Selecting Your Oils

When selecting your oils, it's best to keep in mind the magickal properties each oil has. A sweet scent works great to attract love, and earthy scents aid in growth and prosperity. On the next page you'll see some basic scents that I use frequently, along with the corresponding magickal properties for each.

Essential Oils

Bergamont: truth, purification, blessing, healing, prosperity, magickal energy.

Eucalyptus: healing, purification, blessing, stop gossip.

Lavender: healing, love, purification, sleep, tranquility, relaxation.

Orange: magickal energy, purification, prosperity.

Patchouly: love, lust, prosperity.

Sandalwood: psychic power, protection, lust, purification, all-purpose.

Ylang Ylang: tranquility, love, lust, dreams, sleep.

Fragrance Oils

Cinnamon: lust, prosperity, magickal energy, psychic power, healing.

Frankincense: purification, blessing, healing, spirituality, relaxation, all-purpose.

Jasmine: love, lust, dreams, sleep, healing.

Musk: lust, healing, prosperity, magickal energy.

Nutmeg: prosperity, magickal energy, psychic power.

Rain: prosperity, purification, magickal energy, blessing, tranquility.

Vanilla: love, lust, sleep, blessing, tranquility, relaxation.

118 *Mixing Your Magickal Oils*

To create a magickal oil, you'll need to set up a temporary work area. Lay down some newspaper, grab a few paper towels (it can get messy at times), and bring out all the necessary tools. Determine your magickal purpose and select your oils accordingly. In a small jar, place two tablespoons of the base oil. With your dropper, add three to four drops of several fragrances and/or essential oils. Place the cap on the jar and shake well. On a small label, name the mixture and date it, then place the label on the jar. That's it—your magickal oil is done!

Part Five

A Witch's Journal & Magickal Record Keeping

Creating Your Own Book of Shadows

A Book of Shadows is a book that each and every Wiccan possesses. This sacred book is created by the Witch and is usually kept in a special place. Secret spells and witchy information are scattered throughout. Every Book of Shadows is unique and special. There is no "one" or "true" Book of

Shadows because there is no "one" or "true" way to access the Wiccan Path.

Out of all my tools, my Book of Shadows is by far the most sacred and special. A good Book of Shadows reflects the practitioner by revealing her journey, hopes, and dreams; it is a place for her to record every ritual and spell she has cast. You may be thinking, *What? Write down every spell? That's going to get complicated.* With the help of two magickal sheets provided at the end of this section, you'll be able to get organized with the snap of your fingers! This section will not only help you create your Book of Shadows, it will provide simple suggestions that will help you keep it organized.

✦ *Making Your Book of Shadows*

Contrary to popular belief, the outside of your Book of Shadows isn't nearly as important as its content (and its neatness!). However, you'll need something sturdy to contain that information. I use a black binder with folders inside the flaps. Using a binder works best because you can easily add and eliminate pages. You may also want to consider using a spiralbound notebook, a diary, or even a leather-bound book. Decorating your book adds a personal touch, and it's fun, too! You could cover notebooks with star wrapping paper, or use stamps and colored pencils to add flair. Whether you dress it up in an ornate fashion or go with a basic and simple design, the choice is yours.

Inside Your Book of Shadows

If you are utilizing the binder method, you have a large selection of paper from which to choose. To start your Book of Shadows you will need about thirty to forty sheets of paper. The best place to buy paper is at your local office supply store. The selection is wonderful: speckled, colored, or parchment—take your pick. Most of the time you can buy individual sheets or a ream (a package containing five hundred sheets of paper). If you are on a tight budget, homemade witchy paper is the next best thing. Using regular printer paper or looseleaf paper, you can decorate the margins with witchy symbols, pictures from magazines, stamps, or colored pencils. If you are a computer buff, you have the power to create your own fabulous personalized paper. Just open up a blank document, experiment with some fonts, slap on an image, and print.

Organizing

Organizing your book isn't that hard if you do it correctly. Dividing the book into different sections provides quick access to important notes. Here is an easy outline for you to follow.

Front Matter

The first page should be a book blessing. The second page can be a short story about how you found the Craft. (If you plan on giving your book to a loved one at a later date, I am sure they'd love to read your story!)

Section One: Journal

This is sometimes referred to as a mirror book because it is a mirror of yourself. Here you write down thoughts, poetry, and spell experiences. It is important to write in your book at least once a week. You'll be able to track your progress and growth. Anything and everything from art to your hopes and dreams will be placed here, sealing your book with love.

Section Two: Basic Wicca

In this section place information you've gathered on Wicca, such as creation myths, ethics, and more.

Section Three: Deity Work—The Goddess and God

Compile a list of ancient deities and their attributes, myths, and stories. Here is a great place to keep favorite invocations, poems, and images of specific deities to whom you relate.

Section Four: Magick Basics and Correspondences

Rules and guidelines of Magick. Write a small paragraph about Magick and what it means to you. Include correspondences and magickal properties of candles, herbs, incense, and oils.

124

Section Five: The Magick Circle, Elements, and Tools

Record or create your favorite method of Circle Casting. You may want to include diagrams of your circle and a checklist of the tools you'll be using to cast (for example, a wand, broom, candles, and so on).

Section Six: Rituals and Spells

In this section you actually write and create spells, so it's an important part. This is the best place to keep your spell outline as well as your ritual and spell sheets (see pages 126–128). In this section, keep every spell you've written; doing so provides easy access to locating past spells! It's a fun way to track your progress throughout the years.

Magickal Record Keeping

Maintaining a magickal record is imperative! The following sheets will help you keep things organized. But more than that, they will allow you to track your progress and write a spell using a few simple steps. The ritual and spell sheet requests three separate pieces of information: (1) the date brewed (when was the spell cast?); (2) the name of the ritual (write the complete name of Sabbat, full moon, or spell); and (3) the reason/for whom (the deity or person for whom the ritual is directed). Fill in one line each time you cast a spell or perform a ritual.

The spell outline works together with the "Eleven Steps to Writing and Casting a Bewitching Spell" (see page 93). The spell outline is created so every bit of information regarding each particular spell can be kept on one page. (You have already seen an example of the spell outline and how it can be utilized in the example following the "Eleven Steps to Writing and Casting a Bewitching Spell.")

Spell Outline

Spell Created: _____

Spell Brewed: _____

(Name of Spell)

Magickal Checklist

Type of Magick: _____

_____

Color Theme: _____

_____

Herbs: _____

_____

Charms: _____

_____

Tools: _____

_____

Best Moon Phase:_____ **127**

_____

Reason/For Whom:_____

_____

Tools/Materials Needed:_____

_____

The Spell:_____

_____

Additional Notes:_____

_____

Results Seen:_____

_____

Ritual and Spell Sheet

Date Brewed   Name of Ritual   Reason/For Whom

1. _____   _____   _____

2. _____   _____   _____

3. _____   _____   _____

4. _____   _____   _____

5. _____   _____   _____

6. _____   _____   _____

7. _____   _____   _____

8. _____   _____   _____

9. _____   _____   _____

10. _____   _____   _____

A farewell Note

Dear friend and Witchling,

I am a teen Wiccan. I know all about the daily grind of a teen's life and the weekly conflicts a teen endures. Let's face it, being a teen is really hard! But being a teenager and a Wiccan practitioner is double trouble! Wicca has the power to change and shape your life—not because Magick will allow you to control others, but because it will allow you to empower and control your own life.

    I sincerely hope you enjoyed this book. By now you've probably cast a spell or two and felt the thrill of Magick course through your veins. Life is filled with Magick . . . maybe you've just never noticed it. Always remember to follow the two rules of Magick and try to apply them to your life every day.

130 If you are a good and kind person, you'll shine in the Goddess' eyes and receive the gifts you've asked for. Whenever you need guidance and love, call to the gods; they will respond in one way or another. When life gets tough and things go wrong, keep faith strong in your heart, and remember . . . there is always hope and tomorrow is a new day.

Some judge a Witch by the title she holds, the number of covens she has belonged to, or the number of years she's been practicing. I have come to realize that a true Witch doesn't need to be told how good she is—she knows it! Each individual possesses personal experiences that can't be judged or rated. So as a Witch, what really matters is the wisdom you've attained, the lessons you've learned, and the inner peace you've maintained. With that in mind, when another Witch judges you or claims your way is "wrong," just smile and be on your way.

Thanks for opening your mind and spirit to me. May the Goddess and God bless you on this magickal path.

Merry Part & Blessed Be
~ Gwinevere Rain ⊛

Appendix: Finding Supplies

Throughout this book I've mentioned a few tools, materials, and supplies that you may want to purchase. At first, finding all of the items may seem a bit daunting, but if you know where to look, you're off to a good start.

To locate a metaphysical/occult (witchy) store in your area, look in the phone book under "New Age" or "metaphysical," search the Internet, ask around, or peek at a current edition of *The Wicca Source Book,* by Gerina Dunwich.

Most metaphysical stores carry herbs such as dragon's blood, special crystals like hematite, and charcoals used with magickal (loose) incense mixtures. If you find that there isn't a store near you, the Internet can come in very handy. There are many great metaphysical on-line stores that carry a wide array of products, tools, and supplies.

Most herbs listed in my book can be found in your kitchen cabinet, at the supermarket, or in natural food stores. Most natural food stores carry incense, essential oils, and loose herbs. You may also want to check out their organic foods, lotions, and soaps.

132 You'll find a large selection of candles, satin cords, and fabric (for conjuring bags) at discount stores or in craft stores.

As far as purchasing books, many large bookstores have a New Age/metaphysical section containing a wonderful selection of witchy books. Also, check out the Further Reading section for some great books that I recommend.

Further Reading

If you'd like to learn more about this path, read some of the following books:

Wicca

Cunningham, Scott. *Living Wicca: A Further Guide for the Solitary Practitioner*. St. Paul, Minn.: Llewellyn Publications, 1993.

———. *Wicca: A Guide for the Solitary Practitioner*. St. Paul, Minn.: Llewellyn Publications, 1988.

Hawke, Elen. *In the Circle: Crafting the Witches' Path*. St. Paul, Minn.: Llewellyn Publications, 2000.

———. *The Sacred Round: A Witch's Guide to Magical Practice*. St. Paul, Minn.: Llewellyn Publications, 2002.

Horne, Fiona. *Witch: A Magickal Journey*. Hammersmith, London: Thorsons, 2001.

Monaghan, Patricia. *Wild Girls*. St. Paul, Minn.: Llewellyn Publications, 2001.

West, Kate. *The Real Witches' Handbook*. Hammersmith, London: Thorsons, 2001.

Magick and Spell Books

Baker, Marina. *Spells for Teenage Witches*. Berkeley, Calif.: Seastone, 2000.

Cunningham, Scott. *Magical Aromatherapy*. St. Paul, Minn.: Llewellyn Publications, 1989.

———. *Magical Herbalism*. St. Paul, Minn.: Llewellyn Publications, 1982.

Dubats, Sally. *Natural Magick.* New York: Citadel Press, 1999.

RavenWolf, Silver. *Teen Witch Kit.* St. Paul, Minn.: Llewellyn Publications, 2000.

Sabrina, Lady. *The Witch's Master Grimoire.* Franklin Lakes, N.J.: New Page Books, 2000.

Telesco, Patricia. *A Victorian Grimoire.* St. Paul, Minn.: Llewellyn Publications, 1998.

Glossary of Witchy Words

Altar: A small designated area in which Wiccans place tools, statues, candles, and other things for the purpose of working Magick and worshipping the Gods.

Book of Shadows: A Wiccan's journal that contains spells, formulas, rituals, and correspondences.

Broom Closet: A symbolic place that represents Wiccans who choose to hide their religious beliefs from others. Most of the time people reside in the broom closet because they fear religious discrimination and persecution.

Consecration: To bless and rid negative energies.

Corners: The four cardinal directions—north, east, south, and west. In Magick, each corner has a corresponding element. The corners are placed within the circle and are invoked during Circle Castings.

Correspondences: Magickal properties of specific herbs, oils, incense, and so on. (For example, roses can be used in love spells because they contain loving properties.)

Coven: A group of three or more practitioners who gather together to cast Magick, celebrate holidays, and perform full moon rituals.

Deosil: Moving in a clockwise motion. Witches move deosil when casting the Magick circle.

Divination: A magickal art of discovering unanswered questions. Some examples of divination are tarot, runes, and the pendulum. See the section about tools for more information about divination.

Grimoire: A workbook containing witchy information. A Grimoire is mainly for spells, rituals, and formulas, as opposed to a Book of Shadows, which can also be a Witch's journal.

Invocation (Invoke): An appeal or petition to higher powers. A prayer to the gods.

Karma: The belief that the actions we take and the energies we send out will return to us in the future. Buddhists believe that karma will be returned in the next lifetime. Wiccans believe that karma will be returned sometime during the current lifetime, and with three times the energy.

Magick: The art of using positive energy to focus your will and create positive and useful change.

Magick Circle: Mentally projected protection sphere. The purpose of the Magic circle is to protect the practitioner and aid in concentration.

Offering: A gift of thanks to the gods. Offerings are tokens of gratitude such as something handmade, a special rock or shell, a drawing, a poem, and so on. Offerings contain no blood sacrifices.

Pentacle: A five-point star with a circle around it.

Pentagram: A simple five-point star.

Power Hand: The hand you use when you write.

Premonition: Psychic abilities; foreseeing the future.

Sabbats: The eight Wiccan holidays: Yule (winter solstice); Imbolc; Ostara (vernal/spring equinox); Beltane; Midsummer (summer solstice); Lammas; Mabon (autumnal/fall equinox); and Samhain. The sabbats are collectively referred to as "Wheel of the Year" because the seasons and Sabbats work in cycle.

Solitary: An individual who practices Witchcraft by herself.

Spell: The use of magickal energy in conjunction with physical tools. Each spell contains the use of visualization, a specific magickal desire, a chant or incantation, an action, and Magickal tools such as a candle, a poppet, or a conjuring bag.

Visualization: Mentally focusing on a specific object or desired result.

Wicca: A pagan religion whose practitioners believe in Goddesses and Gods. Wiccans strive for spiritual empowerment.

Wiccan: A practitioner of the religion of Wicca. Sometimes referred to as a Witch.

Witchcraft: The art and practice of Magick.

Witches' Rune: The pentacle.

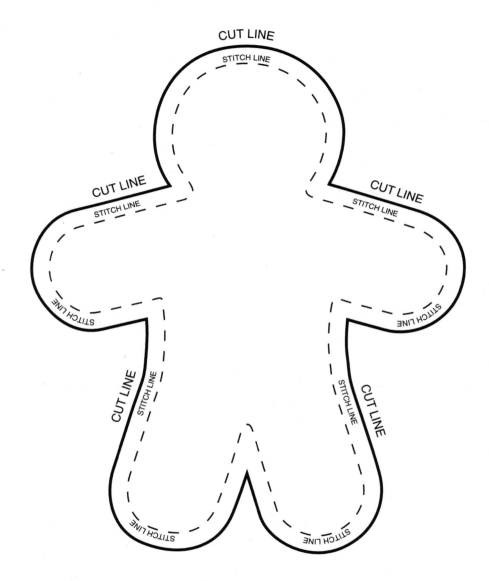

Poppet pattern

Notes

_____

_____

_____

_____

_____

_____

_____

_____

We'd Love to Hear from You . . .

Got ideas?

Llewellyn would love to know what kinds of books you are looking for but can't seem to find. Witchy, occult, paranormal, metaphysical, New Age—what do you want to know about? What types of books will speak specifically to you? What New Age subject areas do you feel need to be covered? If you have ideas, suggestions, or comments, write to Megan at:

megana@llewellyn.com

Llewellyn Publications
Attn: Megan, Acquisitions
P.O. Box 64383-0383
St. Paul, MN 55164-0383 USA
1-800-THE MOON (1-800-843-6666)